DATA STRUCTURE USING C++

DATA STRUCTURE USING C++

By

N. Jayalakshmi

MCA, M.Phil., (PhD),
Dept. of Computer Applications,
Senior Lecturer,
Velammal College of Management and Computer Studies,
Chennai (Tamil Nadu)

FIREWALL MEDIA

(An Imprint of Laxmi Publications Pvt. Ltd.)

BANGALORE • CHENNAI • COCHIN • GUWAHATI • HYDERABAD
JALANDHAR • KOLKATA • LUCKNOW • MUMBAI • RANCHI
NEW DELHI • BOSTON, USA

Published by :
FIREWALL MEDIA
(*An Imprint of Laxmi Publications Pvt. Ltd.*)
113, Golden House, Daryaganj,
New Delhi-110002

Phone : 011-43 53 25 00
Fax : 011-43 53 25 28
www.laxmipublications.com
info@laxmipublications.com

Price : **Rs. 95.00** *Only.*

First Edition : 2007
Reprint : 2009

OFFICES

India

✆ **Bangalore**	080-26 61 15 61
✆ **Chennai**	044-24 34 47 26
✆ **Cochin**	0484-239 70 04
✆ **Guwahati**	0361-254 36 69, 251 38 81
✆ **Hyderabad**	040-24 65 23 33
✆ **Jalandhar**	0181-222 12 72
✆ **Kolkata**	033-22 27 43 84
✆ **Lucknow**	0522-220 95 78
✆ **Mumbai**	022-24 91 54 15, 24 92 78 69
✆ **Ranchi**	0651-221 47 64

USA

Boston
11, Leavitt Street, Hingham,
MA 02043, USA

FDA-2872-095-DATA STRUCTURE USING C++
C—16803/08/12
Typeset at : Kalyani Computer Services, New Delhi.
Printed at : Sanjeev Offset Printers, Delhi.

CONTENTS

PREFACE

The study of data structures and algorithms is fundamental to computer science and engineering. A mastery of these areas is essential for us to develop computer programs that utilize computer resources in an effective manner. Consequently, all computer science and engineering curriculums include one or more courses devoted to these subjects.

This book provides a comprehensive introduction to the modern study of data structures. It presents many algorithms and covers them in considerable depth, yet makes their design and analysis accessible to all levels of readers. I have tried to keep explanations elementary without sacrificing depth of coverage.

With the emergence of the object-oriented paradigm as the framework of choice for the implementation of robust and reusable software, I have tried to take a consistent object-oriented viewpoint throughout this text. One of the main ideas of the object-oriented approach is that data should be presented as being encapsulated with the methods that access and modify them. That is, rather than simply viewing data as a collection of bytes and addresses, we think of data as instances of an abstract data type (ADT) that includes a repertory of methods for performing operations on the data. Thus, I present each data structure using ADTs and their respective implementations.

The first chapter deals with the concept of ADT. Then the following five chapters are describing the concepts of array, stack, queue, linked list, tree and graph. Seventh chapter is about searching and sorting methods. Efficient search trees are explained in the last chapter.

A unique feature of this book is the emphasis on applications. Several real-world applications illustrate the use of each data structure and algorithm-design method developed in this book. Typically, the last section of each chapter is dedicated to applications of the data structure or design method studied earlier in the chapter.

The text is intended primarily for use in undergraduate or graduate courses in data structures. Because it discusses engineering issues in algorithm design, as well as mathematical aspects, it is equally well suited for self-study by technical professionals.

TO THE READERS

I hope that this textbook provides you with an enjoyable introduction to the field of Data Structures. I have attempted to make every algorithm accessible and interesting. To help you when you encounter unfamiliar or difficult algorithms, I describe each one in a step-by-step manner. I have included over 100 exercises and over 30 C++ programs for the data structures and algorithms.

WHAT ARE THE PREREQUISITES FOR READING THIS BOOK?

I have written this book assuming that the reader comes to it with certain knowledge. Namely, I assume that the reader is at least vaguely familiar with a high-level programming language, such as C and C++.

—AUTHOR

1

INTRODUCTION TO DATA STRUCTURES

1.1 WHAT IS DATA STRUCTURE?

Data structure is the study of how the information is organized in a computer, how it can be manipulated and how it can be utilized.

When we solve the problem with the help of the computer, we are confronted with the following problems:

1. The relationship between the data elements.
2. Operations performed on the logically related data elements.
3. Representation of data elements in the memory.
4. What programming language can be adopted to implement the operations on the data?

Data in a particular problem consists of a set of elementary data items. The possible ways in which the data items are logically related define different data structures.

The representation of particular data structure in the memory is called a storage structure. A particular data structure can have many possible memory configurations or data structures. For example, the array can be implemented in many number of storage structures. In a same way, more than two data structures to be represented by the same data structure. For example, stack and queue can be represented in sequential and non-sequential representations.

The fourth problem tells, if the representation of data structure does not exist in the programming language, the program may be quite complex. But the programmer can write the program to construct and manipulate the data structures.

The data structures, their associated storage structures, the operations on data structures and the problem solving aspects through C++ will be examined in detail in this text.

1.2 ALGORITHM ANALYSIS

It is necessary to analyze the algorithm of a problem after developing. One way of analysis is to check the logical correctness and implementation through testing.

Another type of analysis is its simplicity. The algorithm might be expressed in a simpler way but this simpler approach involves more computer time or space. So when we write the algorithm it is important to be able to analyze the time and space requirements of an algorithm to see if it is in the acceptable limits.

1.2.1 Space Complexity

The Space complexity of a program is the amount of memory it needs to run for completion.

Why space complexity?

- In a multi user computer system, we may need to specify the amount of memory to be allocated.
- In advance we can check whether or not sufficient memory is available to run the program.
- The programmer according to the memory availability can select system s/w programs or language processors.
- To estimate the size of the largest problem that a program can solve.

Components of space complexity are defined as follows:

Instruction space

It is the space to store all the constants and variables. It has the following components.

(*i*) Space needed by constants.

(*ii*) Space needed by variables, arrays, structures and dynamically allocated memory.

Environment stack space

It is used to save information needed to resume execution of partially completed functions.

The space requirement S(P) of any program may be written as

$$S(P) = C + S_p \text{ (Instance characteristics)}$$

Where C is the constant that denotes the fixed part of the space requirements and S_p denotes the variable component for dynamically allocated space and recursion stack space.

1.2.2 Time Complexity

The time complexity of program is the amount of time it needs to run for compilation.

Why time complexity?

- We have to fix up the time limit for a program to avoid indefinite use of computer time.
- Programs designed for interactive use must provide real time response. From the time complexity of a program we can decide whether the program or a program module needs to be redesigned. If it falls on acceptable limit it gets more acceptance.

The time complexity of a program is

T(P) = compile time + run time.

The compiled program can be executed several times. So, we have to consider only runtime (Tp). Let n denotes the instance characteristics, then

Tp(n) = Ca ADD(n) + Cs SUB(n) + Cm MUL(n) + Cd DIV(n) + ...

Where Ca denotes the time needed for addition. ADD, SUB, MUL and DIV are functions whose value is the number of operations.

The time needed for operations depends on its data type. So we must separate the operation counts by data type. And count number of operations being performed. The success depends on the ability to identify the operations that contribute most to the time complexity.

1.3 ABSTRACT DATA TYPE

Definition: A set of values and associated operations that are precisely specified independent of any particular implementation. Objects of the type are created and inspected only by calls to the access functions.

For example let us assume the simple ADT stack. The operations on this stack are called as axioms. They are new (), push (v,s), top(s), and popoff(s). The axioms are as follows:

- New () returns a stack.
- Popoff(push(v,s)) = s
- Top (push(v,s)) = v

Where S is a stack and v is a value. From the above axioms we can define some more additional axioms as follows:

- isempty(new()) = true
- isempty(push(v,s)) = false

1.3.1 Abstraction

When we handle problems it is necessary to design abstract view, or model of the problem to the user. This abstraction hides all the unnecessary things from the user and makes the application easier to understand.

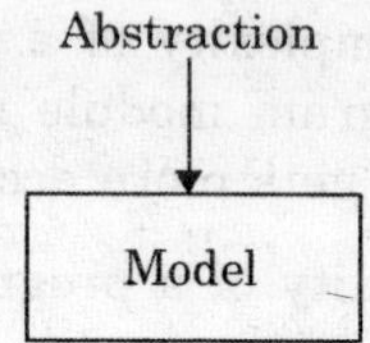

Fig. 1.1 Abstraction

The model focuses only on the following.

- The data, which are affected by the problem.
- The operations, which are identified by the problem.

So abstraction is the structuring of a nebulous problem into well-defined entities by defining their data and operations.

1.3.2 Properties of ADT

With abstraction you create a well-defined entity, which can be properly handled. These entities define the data structure of a set of items. The data structure can only be accessed with defined operations. This set of operations is called interface and is exported by the entity. An entity with the properties just described is called Abstract Data Type (ADT).

The figure 1.2 shows an ADT, which consists of an abstract data structure, and operations only the operations are viewable from outside.

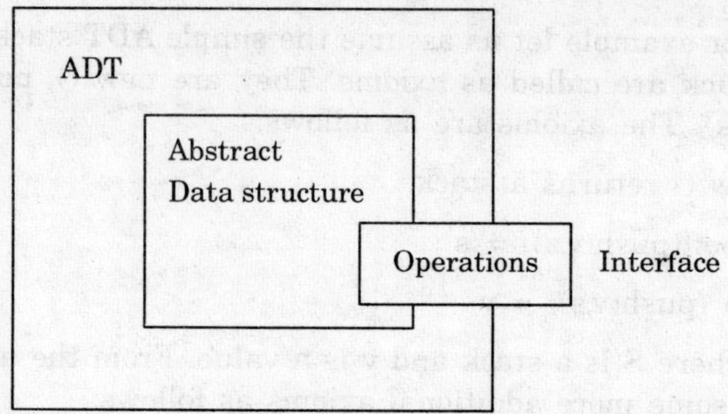

Fig. 1.2 Abstract data structure

The characteristics of ADT are as follows:

1. It exports a type.
2. It exports a set of operations. This set is called interface.

3. Operations of the interface are the one and only access mechanism to the type's of data structure.
4. Axiom and preconditions define the application domain of the type.

1.3.3 ADT Notation

Each ADT description consists of following parts:

- Data: Describes the structures of data used in ADT.
- Operations: Describes valid operations for this ADT.

Example: ADT integer.

Data: Refer the signed whole number as N.

Operations :

Constructor: Creates new integer.

Add (k): Creates new integer, which is sum of N and K.

Sub (k): Creates new integer, which is the difference between N and K.

Set (k): Set N to K.

...

ADT and Object orientation :

ADT allows the creation of instances with well-defined properties and behavior. In object orientation ADT's are referred to as classes. Therefore a class defines properties of objects, which are instances in an object-oriented environment.

Exercises

1. What is time-space trade off ?
2. Analyze the computing time and worse case runtime for function sort.
3. Derive an ADT for floating point number.

2

ARRAYS

2.1 GENERAL LISTS

A list is an ordered set consisting of a variable number of elements to which insertions and deletions can be made. If the elements of lists are adjacent to one another it is said to be linear.

The operations of the list include addition, deletion, modification and retrieval of an element. The size of the list can be modified for addition and specifying its position can do deletion and also the operations.

Each element is a list composed of one or more fields. Other than addition and deletion operations the following operations can be done on element of list.

1. Combine two or more lists from another list.
2. Split the list into number of other lists.
3. Copy a list.
4. Determine the number of elements in a list.
5. Sort the elements of list into ascending or descending order.
6. Search a list for an element which contains a field having a certain value.

These operations will be discussed for various structures throughout this book.

A file is typically a large list stored in the external memory of a computer.

2.2 ARRAY

An array is an ordered set, which consists of a fixed number of objects. Deletion and insertion operations are not performed on arrays. The elements can be accessed or the elements can be modified.

2.2.1 ADT of an Array

Each instance of the data object array is a set of pairs of the form (index, value). No two pairs in this set have the same index.

ADT Array

{

Instances

set of (index, value) pairs, no two pairs have the same index.

Operations:

Create (): Create an empty array.

Store (index, value): add this pair to set deleting existing pair (if any). With the same index

Retrieve (index): return the pair with this index value.

}

Example:

The rainfall in mm in metro cities can be represented as

Rain = { (Delhi,70), (Chennai, 5), (Mumbai, 30), (Kolkata, 0) }

Each pair has an index (name of the city) and value (rainfall in mm). We can change the rainfall recorded for Chennai to 8 by performing the operation.

Store (Chennai, 8)

We can determine rainfall in Kolkata by performing.

Retrieve (Kolkata)

The names of the city can be assigned with index values (0, 1.......4), which replaces (Delhi.........Kolkata)

2.2.2 Storage Representation for Array

One-dimensional array

A one-dimensional array is used when it is necessary to keep a large number of items in memory and reference all the items in a uniform manner. Normally, a number of memory locations is sequentially allocated to the vector. An array size is fixed so it requires a fixed number of memory locations.

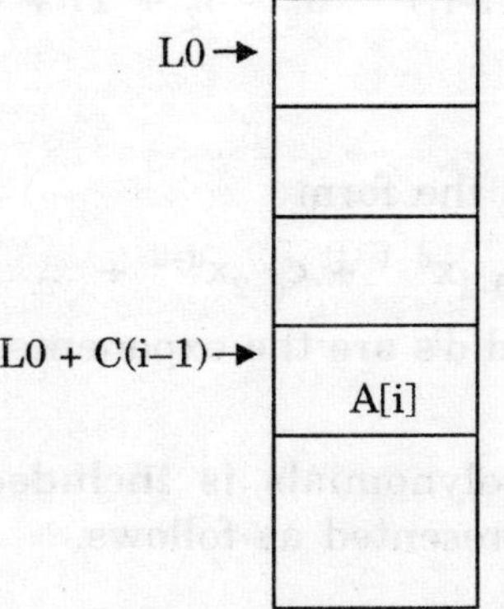

Fig. 2.1 Array

Let us assume the address of the first word of the array A is L0, and C represents the number of words allocated to each element. The address of the element A_i is given by

Loc (A_i) = L0 + C * (i–1).

If the lower boundary of the array is b, then

Loc (A_i) = L0 + C * (i–b).

Multi-dimensional array

A multi-dimensional array can be represented by an equivalent one-dimensional array. For example, a two dimensional array consisting of two rows and three columns is stored sequentially by columns as

A[1,1], A[2,1], A[1,2], A[2,2], A[1,3], A[2,3]

↑

L0

The address of element A [i,j] can be evaluated as

Loc (A[i,j] = Lo + (j–1)2 + i–1

If the array of size A (m,n) the location of A[i,j] can be evaluated by the equation

Loc (A[i,j] = Lo + (j–1)n + (i–1)

In many programming languages, a two-dimensional array will be stored row by row (row _ major order). The representation such order will be

A[1,1], A[1,2], A[1,3], A[2,1], A[2,2], A[2,3]

The address of element A [i,j] of size m × n is given by the expression

Loc (A[i,j] = Lo + (j–1) * m + (j–1)

The representation of two-dimensional array with arbitrary lower and upper boundaries like $l_1 \leq i \leq u_1$ and $l_2 \leq i \leq u_2$. The location of A [i,j] is given by

$$\text{Loc (A [i,j]} = \text{Lo} + (i-l_1) * (u_2 - l_2 + 1) + (j-l_2)$$

2.3 POLYNOMIALS

A polynomial of degree d has the form

$$c_d x^d + c_{d-1} x^{d-1} + c_{d-2} x^{d-2} + \ldots.. + c_0$$

The c_is are coefficient and d's are the exponents. Each c_i x_i is a term of the polynomial.

The manipulation on polynomials is included in the ADT of a polynomial, which can be represented as follows.

```
Class poly
{
```

Objects:

Set of ordered pairs of exponents and coefficients.

Operations:

Poly ( ) : creates an empty polynomial.

Coefficient coeff(Exponent e) : returns a coeff of a given e.

Exponent Load exp( ) : returns largest exponent of a polynomial.

Poly Add (poly P): returns the sum of * this and P.

Poly mult (poly P): returns the product of * this and P.

float Eval (float p): Evaluate poly at f and returns the value.

}

2.3.1 Polynomials Representation

When we represent the polynomial in memory if the exponents are in descending order, it is more useful for the operations. There are three different representations for the polynomial described as follows.

Representation–1

Declaration of the private data members of the polynomial is

```
Private:
int degree;    // degree ≤ Max degree
float coef [Maxdegree + 1];
```

Where Max degree is a constant representing largest degree polynomial that is to be represented. The polynomial A(x) can be represented as

a.degree = n

a.coeff[i] = a_{n-1} , 0<i<n.

a.coeff[i] is the co-eff of x_{n-i}, the coefficient are stored in order of decreasing components.

Representation–2

The private data members are declared as follows in order to avoid wastage of memory in Representation–1.

```
Private:
int degree;
float *coeff;
```

and the constructor of the polynomial is

```
Poly :: Poly( int n)
{
degree = d;
coeff = new float [degree+1];
}
```

Representation–3

The second representation also wastes the memory for the exponents which the coefficient zeros. Let us consider the polynomial x1000 + 1. Which has only two non-zero coefficients. Remaining 999 locations will be free when we use second representation. To avoid this problem we can have coefficient and exponent in the array, whose size can be defined during run time.

Program for polynomial addition

```
#include<iostream.h>
#include<conio.h>
#include<stdio.h>
class poly;
class term
{
    int exp;
    int coff;
    friend poly;
};
class poly
{
    int n,i;
    term *t;
    public:
    poly(int x)
    {
        n=x;
        t = new term[n];
        i=0;
    }
    poly add(poly);
    void create(int,int);
    void print();
};
void poly::create(int x,int y)
{
    t[i].coff = x;
    t[i].exp= y;
    i++;
}
```

```
void poly::print()
{
    for(int i=0;i<n;i++)
    {
        if(t[i].coff>0)
        cout<<"+"<<t[i].coff<<"X^"<<t[i].exp;
        else
        cout<<t[i].coff<<"X^"<<t[i].exp;
    }
}
poly poly::add(poly b)
{
    poly c(n+b.n);
    i=0;
    b.i=0;
    c.i=0;
    while( i<n && b.i<b.n)
    {
        if(t[i].exp == b.t[b.i].exp)
        {
            .create(t[i].coff+b.t[b.i].coff,t[i].exp);
            i++;
            .i++;
            .n--;
        }
        else if(t[i].exp < b.t[b.i].exp)
        {
            .create(b.t[b.i].coff,b.t[b.i].exp);
            .i++;
        }
        else
        {
            .create(t[i].coff,t[i].exp);
            i++;
        }
    }
    if(i==n)
```

```
        {
            for(;b.i<b.n;b.i++)
            c.create(b.t[b.i].coff,b.t[b.i].exp);
        }
        if(b.i==b.n)
        {
            for(;i<n;i++)
            c.create(t[i].coff,t[i].exp);
        }
      return(c);
    }
  void main()
    {
        int c,e;
        int m,n;
        clrscr();
        cout<<"\t\tPolynomial Addition\n";
        cout<<"\t\t~~~~~~~~~~~ ~~~~~~~~~\n\n";
        cout<<"Enter the size of First Polynomial\n";
        cin>>m;
        cout<<"Enter the size of Second Polynomial\n";
        cin>>n;
        poly A(m),B(n),C(m+n);
        for(int i=0;i<m;i++)
        {
            cout<<"Enter the coff & exp first Poly \n";
            cin>>c>>e;
            A.create(c,e);
        }
        for(i=0;i<n;i++)
        {
            cout<<"Enter the coff & exp of second poly\n";
            cin>>c>>e;
            B.create(c,e);
        }
      cout<<"\nFirst Polynomial is :\n";
      cout<<"\t";A.print();
```

```
cout<<"\nSecond Polynomial is :\n";
cout<<"\t";B.print();
 C=A.add(B);
cout<<"\nResultant Polynomial is :\n";
cout<<"\t";C.print();
 getch();
}
```

2.4 SPARSE MATRIX

A matrix, which has more number of zero elements, is called sparse matrix. They are commonly used in scientific applications and contain hundreds or even thousand of rows and columns. The sequential representation operations become inefficient.

Consider a matrix

$$\begin{bmatrix} 5 & 0 & 0 & 0 & 2 & 0 \\ 0 & 0 & 3 & 0 & 0 & 0 \\ 0 & -7 & 0 & 0 & 0 & 1 \\ 0 & 0 & 0 & 0 & 0 & 2 \\ 0 & 0 & 0 & -6 & 0 & 0 \\ 0 & 0 & 0 & 0 & -8 & 0 \end{bmatrix}$$

Fig. 2.2 Representation of sparse matrix (6 × 6)

In which out of 36 elements only 8 elements are non zero. Even though there is no precise definition of sparse matrix the above matrix can be called as sparse since it has very few non-zero elements.

When we deal with large matrices like 2000 × 2000 elements and consider it is sparse. If we store all the elements in the memory, the efficiency of the system will be poor. So, we can go for alternative way of storing the sparse, which stores only non zero elements.

2.4.1 ADT of a Sparse Matrix

Before considering the representation of sparse matrix, let us create an ADT. The set of operations on sparse matrix includes matrix creation, transportation, addition and multiplication.

```
Class sparse matrix
{
//objects : set of row, column and value
public :
sparse matrix(int maxrow, int maxcol)
//constructor
```

```
sparse matrix Transpose( );
// returns a transpose sparse matrix
sparse matrix Add( sparse matrix b)
//adds the and b and returns the result
sparse matrix multiply (sparse matrix b)
}
```

2.4.2 Sparse Matrix Representation

Each element of the array is a triple (row, column, value). Normally the matrix will be stored in column major order. So the column indices are in ascending order. In addition to that to operate on the matrices we must know the number of rows, number of columns and number of non-zero elements in the array.

The array in fig. 2.3 can be represented as

Smatrix

	Row	Column	Value
[0]	0	0	5
[1]	0	4	2
[2]	1	2	3
[3]	2	1	-7
[4]	2	5	1
[5]	3	5	2
[6]	4	3	-6
[7]	5	4	-8

Fig. 2.3 Sparse matrix

We define the sparse matrix as follows.

```
Class matrix term
{
friend class Sparse matrix ;
private :
int row, col, value;
}
class sparse matrix
{
int rows, cols, terms;
matrix term *smatrix;
public :
// operations on sparse matrices
}
```

Matrix is an array, which holds the triples of non-zero elements. This array will be allocated during runtime according to the value of terms.

Rows and cols are the variables represent the number of rows and columns of the sparse matrix.

2.4.3 Transpose Matrix

Fig. 2.4 shows the transpose of matrix in fig. 2.3 to transpose a matrix, we must interchange the rows and columns. Since the matrix is stored in row major order to transpose we can do the following.

For (each row i)

take element (i, j, value) and

store it in (j, i, value) of the transpose;

Fig. 2.4 shows that the movement of triples as per the above for loop. If we place them as it is not possible to search the element easily because it is not in ascending order. We can avoid this data movement by finding the elements in the order we want them, which would be

for (all elements in column j)

place element (i, j, value) in postion (j, i, value);

	R	C	V
Smatrix	0	0	5
	4	0	2
	2	1	3
	1	2	–7
	5	2	1
	5	3	2
	3	4	–6
	4	5	–8

R	C	V
0	0	4
1	2	–7
2	1	3
3	4	–6
4	0	2
4	5	–8
5	2	5
5	3	2

Fig. 2.4 Transpose matrix

Program for Transpose of Sparse Matrix

```
#include<stdio.h>
#include<conio.h>
#include<iostream.h>
class spa;
class spat
{
        int row,col,value;
        friend spa;
};
class spa
{
        int rows,cols,item;
```

```
        spat *sary;
        public:
        spa tran();
        void print();
        void create(int r,int c,int v);
        spa(int r,int c,int t)
        {
                rows = r;
                cols = c;
                item = t;
                sary = new spat[item];
        }
    };
    void spa::create(int r,int c,int v)
    {
        static int i=0;
        sary[i].row = r;
        sary[i].col = c;
        sary[i].value = v;
        i++;
    }
    void spa::print()
    {
        for(int i=0;i<item;i++)
        {
            cout<<sary[i].row<<"          "<<sary[i].col<<"
        "<<sary[i].value<<"\n";
        }
    }
    spa spa::tran()
    {
        spa b(cols,rows,item);
        int bloc=0;
        for(int c=0;c<cols;c++)
        {
            for(int i=0;i<item;i++)
            {
```

```
                if(sary[i].col == c)
                {
                    b.sary[bloc].row = sary[i].col;
                    b.sary[bloc].col = sary[i].row;
                    b.sary[bloc].value = sary[i].value;
                    bloc++;
                }
            }
        }
        return(b);
    }
void main()
{
    int r,c,t;
    int ro,co,value;
    clrscr();
    printf("Enter the value of r,c t\n");
    cin>>r>>c>>t;
    spa a(r,c,t);
    for(int i=0;i<t;i++)
    {
        cout<<"Value for ro co value\n";
        cin>>ro>>co>>value;
        a.create(ro,co,value);
    }
    spa b(c,r,t);
    b=a.tran();
    cout<<"A sparsc matrix is :\n";
    a.print();
    cout<<"Transpose matrix is:\n";
    b.print();
    getch();
}
```

Exercises

1. How single dimensional arrays are initialized?
2. How many values can be held by an array with dimensions a[0 ... n], b [–1,... n], c[–n ... 0] [1 ... 2]?
3. Write a function String : frequency that determines the frequency of occurrence of each of the distinct characters in the string. Test your function with suitable data.
4. Write a C++ program to find a second maximum of two dimensional array.
5. Write a C++ function to delete duplicate elements.
6. Differentiate array and list.
7. Differentiate array and pointers.
8. Rewrite polynomial addition program using linked list.

3

STACKS AND QUEUES

Stacks and queues are the most frequently used data structures. The stack data structure is obtained from a linear list by restricting the insertions and deletions to take place from the same end. In a queue insertions and deletions take place from different ends of the linear list. This chapter deals with the representation, operations and applications of stack and queue.

3.1 STACK

A stack is a linear list in which insertions and deletions take place at the same end. This end is called the top. The other end of the list is called bottom.

Fig. 3.1 shows a stack with four elements

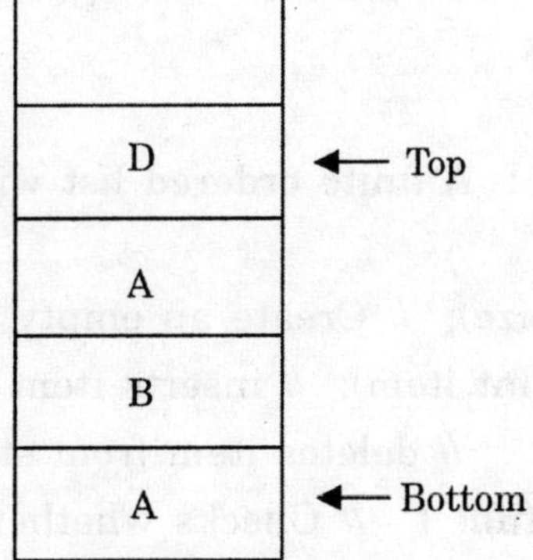

Fig. 3.1 Stack

3.1.1 Operations on Stacks

The insertion operation is referred to as 'Push' and the deletion as 'Pop'. Since the insertion and deletion operations are performed at one end of the stack, the elements can only be removed in the opposite order from that in which they were added to the stack. This phenomenon is called Last In First Out (LIFO).

Fig. 3.2 shows the example of addition and deletion of elements into the stack in fig. 3.1.

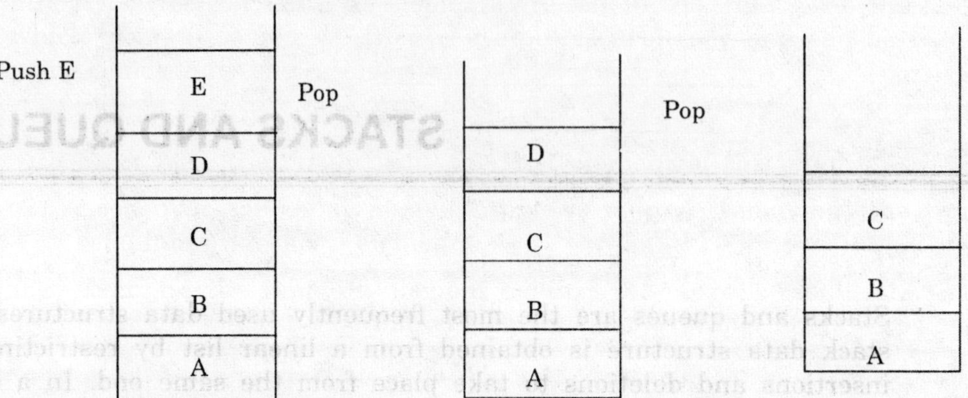

Fig. 3.2 Addition and deletion of elements

A pointer top keeps the track of the top element in the stack. Initially top has a value zero and it will be incremented by 'one' when the element is pushed into a stack. The pointer is decremented by 'one' each time a deletion is made.

3.1.2 The Stack Abstract Date Type

The set of operation on the stack includes insert an item, delete an item, check for stack full or empty. These are given in the ADT specification.

```
Class Stack
{
    // Object : A finite ordered list with zero or more elements.
    Public :
  Stack(int size); // Create an empty stack
  Void Push(int item); // inserts item into the stack
  Int Pop( )      // deletes item from stack
  Boolean Isfull( )  // Checks whether the stack is full
  Boolean Isempty( ) // Checks whether the stack is empty
};
```

3.1.3 Representing Stack in C++

Before programming a stack operation, we must decide how to represent a stack using the data structures that exist in our programming language. There are several ways to represent a stack in C++. Now we consider the simplest representation and which uses the minimum number of memory locations.

```
Class Stack
{
```

```
int top;
int maxsize;
int * stack;
public :   // operations
}
```

The above stack stores only the integer data in it. If you want to change the type of data elements, the data type of stack can be changed.

3.1.4 Push and Pop Operations in C++

To add an element to a stack, we need to increase stack pointer by one and place the new element at S[top]. When we insert we have to check stack pointer for maxsize-1, at this point the stack is full. When we delete an element the stack pointer needs to be decremented by one after deleting S[top]. A stack is empty if stack pointer is equal to zero. We need to check for this condition before deletion.

Program for Stack Implementation

```
#include<iostream.h>
#include<stdio.h>
#include<conio.h>
#include<process.h>
class stack
{
    int *a,top,s;
    public:
    stack(){}
    stack(int);
    void push(int);
    void print();
    int pop();
};
void stack::stack(int n)
{
    s = n;
    a = new int[s];
    top = 0;
}
void stack::push(int item)
{
    if(top == s)
```

```
        {
                cout<<"Stack is full\n";
        }
        else
        {
                top++;
                a[top]=item;
        }
}
int stack::pop()
{
        if(top<0)
        {
                cout<<"Stack is empty\n";
                return 0;
        }
        else
        {
                int i=a[top];
                top--;
                return i;
        }
}
void stack::print()
{
        for(int i=1;i<=top;i++)
        {
                cout<<a[i]<<"\t";
        }
}
void main()
{
    int si,ch;
    int el,c;
    clrscr();
    cout<<"Enter the size of the stack\n";
    cin>>si;
```

```
        stack a(si);
        do
        {
            cout<<"\n\t\t\tMenu\n";
            cout<<"\t\t\t1.Push\n";
            cout<<"\t\t\t2.Pop\n";
            cout<<"\t\t\t3.Print\n";
            cout<<"\t\t\t4.Exit\n";
            cout<<"\tEnter your choice\n";
            cout<<"\t";cin>>ch;
            switch(ch)
            {
                case 1:
                        {
                        cout<<"Enter the element\n";
                        cin>>el;
                        a.push(el);
                        break;
                        }
                case 2:
                        {
                        c = a.pop();
                        cout<<"Delete the elements is :"<<c;
                        break;
                        }
                case 3:
                        {
                        a.print();
                        break;
                        }
                case 4:
                        {
                        exit(0);
                        }
                default:
                        {
                        exit(0);
```

```
            }
        }
    }while(ch<=4);
    getch();
}
```

3.1.5 Applications of Stack

This section contains the applications of stack. The first application deals with recursion, which is an important facility available in many programming languages. The second application of a stack deals with complication of infix expression in to object code and evaluation of expression.

3.1.5.1 Recursion

Recursion is the name given to the technique of defining a set or a process in terms of itself.

The factorial function whose domain is the natural numbers, can be recursively defined as

$$\text{Factorial (N)} = \begin{cases} 1 \text{ if } N = 0 \\ N * \text{factorial (N–1), 0 otherwise} \end{cases}$$

Here factorial (N) is defined in terms of factorial (N–1), which in turn is defined in terms of factorial (N–2) etc. until factorial (0) is reached whose value is 'one'.

An interative process can be illustrated with the flow chart given in fig. 3.3. There are four parts in the process called initialization, decision, computation and update.

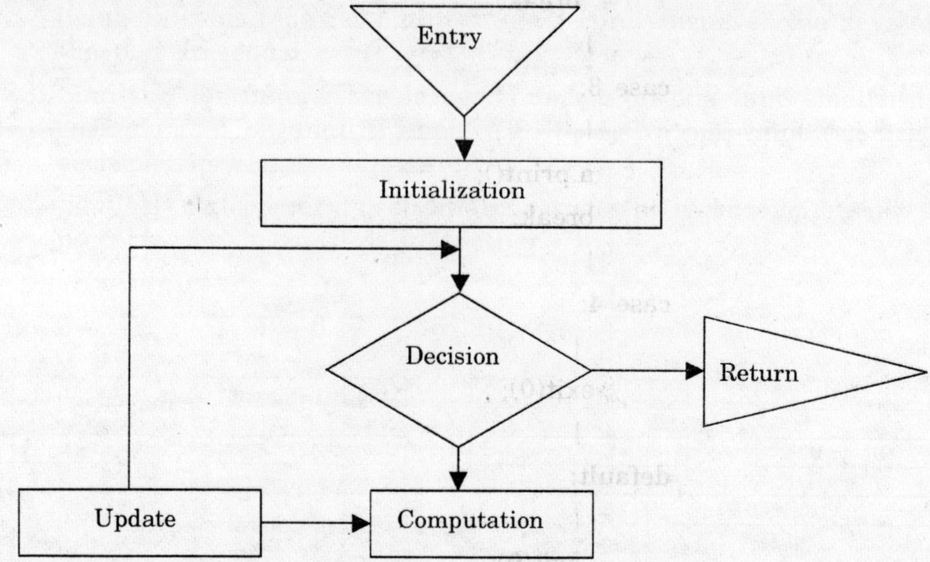

Fig. 3.3 Flowchart for an interative process.

1. Initialization: The parameters of the function and the decision parameter are set to their initial values.
2. Decision: The decision parameter is used to determine whether to remain in the loop.
3. Computation: The required computation is performed.
4. Update: The decision parameter is updated and a transfer to the next iteration.

A recursive procedure can be called from within or outside itself, and to ensure its proper functions, it has to save the return address in some order so that a return to proper location will result when return to a calling statement is made. The procedure must also save the formal parameters local variables, etc., upon entry and restore these parameters and variables at completion.

The recursive procedure contains the following steps.

1. Save the parameters, local variables and return address.
2. If the base criterion has been reached, then perform final computation and go to step-3; otherwise perform partial computation and go to step-1.
3. Restore the most recently stored parameters local variables and return address. Go to this return address.

Note that when the base criterion has been reached, the most recently saved parameters; local variables and return address are restored.

The last in first out characteristic of a recursive procedure suggests that a stack is the most obvious data structure to it. At each procedure call (or level of recursion) the stack is pushed to save the necessary values; while exit from that level, the stack is popped to restore the saved values of the preceding level.

3.1.5.2 *Evaluation of expression*

The compiler cannot accept an expression in infix notation and produce correct code. So the infix expression must be converted into postfix expression, which can be accepted by the compiler. The postfix form of an expression calls for each operator to appear after its operands.

For example

Infix A + B * C has

Postfix ABC * +

In the above postfix expression + Comes after * because * has higher precedence than +. So B*C has to be evaluated and stored in T and then A can be added with it.

So before evaluation of the expression it has to be converted into postfix form. A general form for the conversion process might take the following steps:

1. Initialize stack contents to the special symbol #.
2. Scan the leftmost symbol in the given infix expression and denote it as the current input symbol.
3. Repeat through step-6 while the current input symbol is not #.
4. Remove and output all stack symbols whose procedure values are greater than or equal to the precedence of the current input symbols.
5. Push the current input symbol on to the stack.
6. Scan the leftmost symbol in the infix expression and let it be the current input symbol.

For example, since we want A + B * C to yield ABC * +, our algorithm should perform the following sequence of stacking.

Next Token	Stack	Output
None	Empty	None
A	Empty	A
+	+	A
B	+	AB
*	+*	AB
C	+*	ABC
None	+	ABC*
None	Empty	ABC*+

When we are evaluating the expression, the compiler must use the postfix expression. General algorithms for generating assembly language statements from postfix expressions the following:

1. Repeat through step-3 for all characters in the postfix expression.
2. Obtain the current input symbol.
3. If the current input symbol is a variable then push the variable on the stack else remove the two topmost operands from the stack. Generate the sequence of assembly language instructions, which corresponds to the current arithmetic operator stack the intermediate result.

For example when evaluating ABC*+ the stack positions are given as follows.

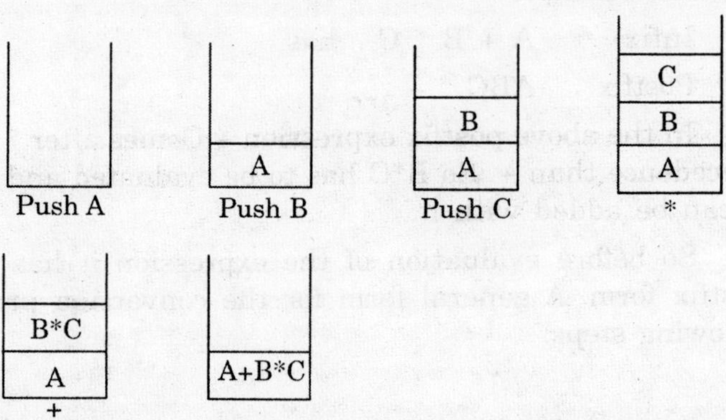

Final result can be taken from top of the stack.

3.2 QUEUE

A queue is an ordered collection of items from which items may be deleted at one end (called the front of the queue) and into which items may be inserted at the other end (called the rear of the queue).

Fig. 3.4 shows the queue with three elements A, B and C. A is at the front of the queue and C is at the rear.

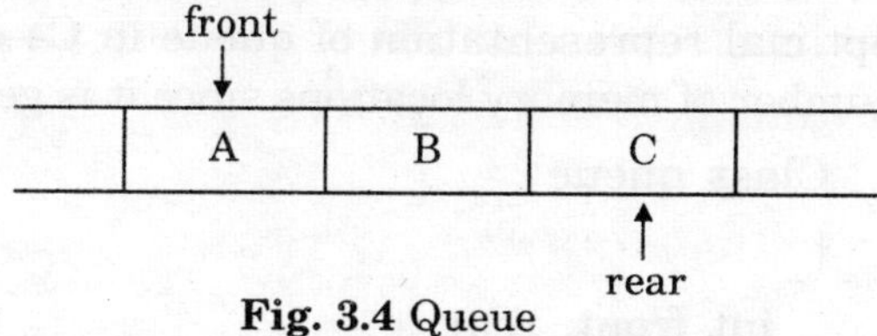

Fig. 3.4 Queue

3.2.1 Linear Queue

The information in a queue is processed in the same order as it was received, that is on a first in first out (FIFO) or First Come First Serve (FCFS) basis. Fig. 3.5 is a representation of a queue illustrating how insertion and deletion made with the help of rear and front.

Insert D:

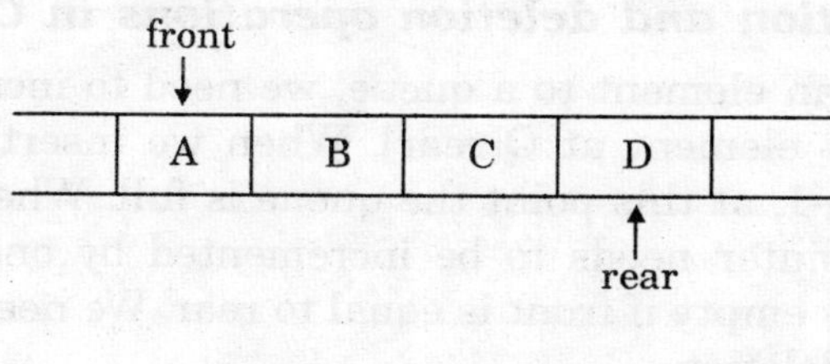

Delete

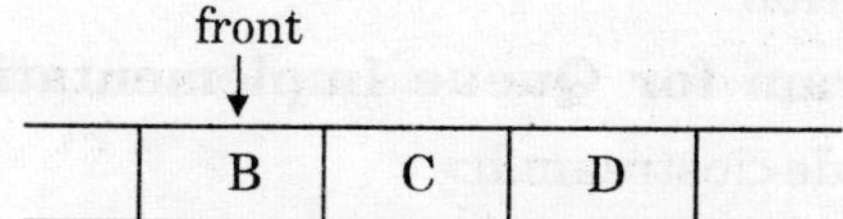

Fig. 3.5 Operations on queues

When we insert the element into a queue the pointer rear gets incremented by one and the new element is placed in queue [rear]. When we want to delete the element the pointer front gets incremented by one after deleting the element from a queue.

3.2.1.1 The queue abstract data type

The set of operations on the queue includes insert an item, delete an item, check for queue full or empty. The ADT specification is as follows

```
Class queue
{
    // object : A finite ordered list with zero or more elements
```

```
Public :
    Queue (int size);  // Creates an empty queue.
    Void insert (int item);  // inserts an item into the queue
    int delete( );  // deletes an item from queue
    Boolean isfull( );  // checks whether the queue is full.
    Boolean isempty( );  // checks whether the queue is empty.
```

3.2.1.2 Representing queue in C++

The optimal representation of queue in C++ is as follows. Which occupies less number of memory locations since it is getting allocated during runtime.

```
Class queue
{
    int front, rear;
    int maxsize;
    int *queue;
    public : // operations.
};
```

The above queue will be getting allocated with integer numbers.

3.2.1.3 Insertion and deletion operations in C++

To add an element to a queue, we need to increase rear by one and place the new element at Q[rear]. When we insert we have to check rear for maxsize-1, at this point the queue is full. When we delete an element the front pointer needs to be incremented by one after deleting Q[front]. A queue is empty if front is equal to rear. We need to check for this condition before deletion.

Program for Queue Implementation

```
#include<iostream.h>
#include<stdio.h>
#include<conio.h>
#include<process.h>

class queue
{
    int *a,front,rear;
    int s;
    public:
    queue(int);
    void push(int);
    void print();
```

```
        int pop();
    };

    void queue::queue(int n)
    {
        s = n;
        a = new int[s];
        front = 0;
        rear = 0;
    }

    void queue::push(int item)
    {
        if(rear == s)
        {
            cout<<"queue is full\n";
        }
        else
        {
            a[rear]=item;
            rear++;
        }
    }

    int queue::pop()
    {
        if(front == rear)
        {
            cout<<"Queue  is empty\n";
            return 0;
        }
        else
        {
            int i=a[front];
            front++;
            return i;
        }
```

```
}

void queue::print()
{
      for(int i=front;i<rear;i++)
      {
            cout<<a[i]<<"\t";
      }
}

void main()
{
  int si,ch;
  int el,c;
  clrscr();
  cout<<"Enter the size of the Queue\n";
  cin>>si;
  queue a(si);
  do
  {
      cout<<"\t\t\tMenu\n";
      cout<<"\t\t\t1.Insert\n";
      cout<<"\t\t\t2.Delete\n";
      cout<<"\t\t\t3.Print\n";
      cout<<"\t\t\t4.Exit\n";
      cout<<"Enter your choice\n";
      cin>>ch;
      switch(ch)
      {
            case 1:
            {
                  cout<<"Enter the element\n";
                  cin>>el;
                  a.push(el);
                  break;
            }
            case 2:
            {
                  c = a.pop();
```

```
                cout<<"Delete the elements is :"<<c;
                break;
            }
            case 3:
            {
                a.print();
                break;
            }
            case 4:
            {
                exit(0);
            }
        }
    }while(ch<=4);
}
```

3.2.2 Circular Queue

The pair of algorithms can be wasteful of storage if the front pointer never manages to catch up to the rear pointer. Actually, an arbitrarily large amount of memory would be required to accommodate the elements.

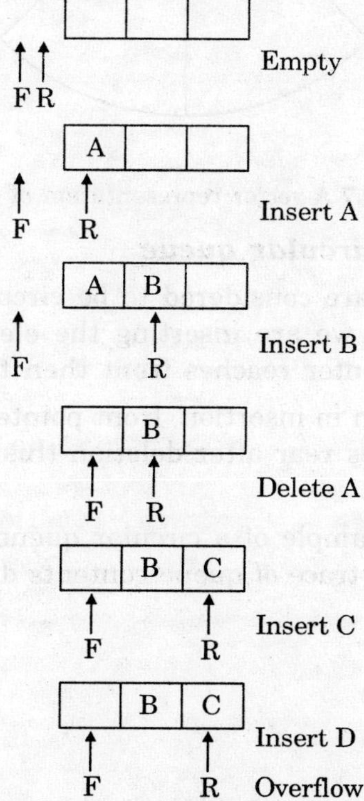

Fig. 3.6 Trace the operations on simple queue

Consider an example where the size of the queue is three elements. Initially the queue is empty. It is required to insert the elements A and B, delete A and insert C and D. A trace given in fig. 3.6 shows the overflow during the insertion of element D, Even though the first location is not being used.

A more suitable method of representing a queue, which prevents an excessive use of memory, is to arrange the elements Q [1], Q [2] .....Q [n] in a circular fashion with Q [1] following Q [n]. Pictorially this can be represented as in fig. 3.7. The insertion and deletion algorithms for a circular queue can now be formulated.

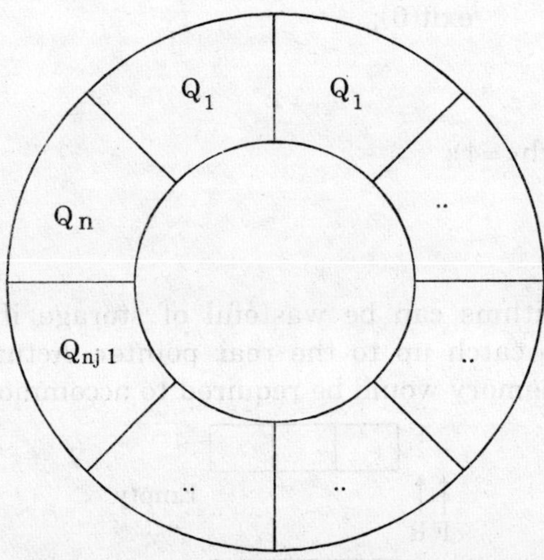

Fig. 3.7 A vector representation of circular queue

3.2.2.1 Operations on circular queue

Since the locations are considered to be circular the rear pointer moves towards front when we are inserting the element in to a queue. While insortion of rear pointer reaches front then the queue becomes full.

As we have seen in insertion, front pointer moves towards rear while deletion. If it reaches rear after deletion this leads to the assumption of empty queue.

Consider an example of a circular queue that contains a maximum of three elements. A trace of queue contents during operations is given in fig. 3.8.

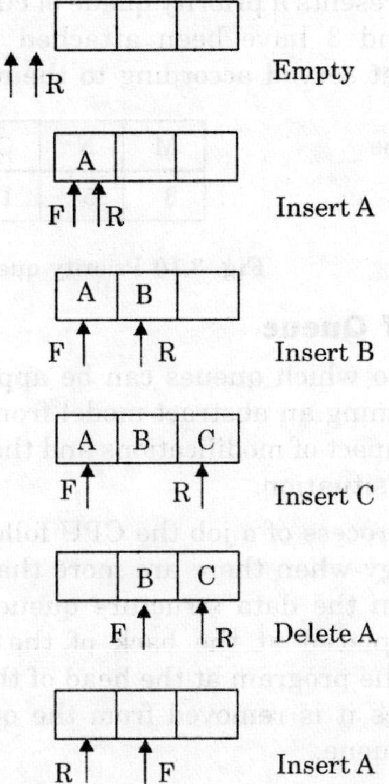

Fig. 3.8 Trace of operations on a circular queue

3.2.3 De Queue

A queue has been described as behaving in a first-in first-out manner in the sense that each deletion removes the oldest remaining item in the structure.

A De queue called double-ended queue is a linear list in which insertions and deletions are made to or from either end of the structure. Fig 3.9 can represent such structure.

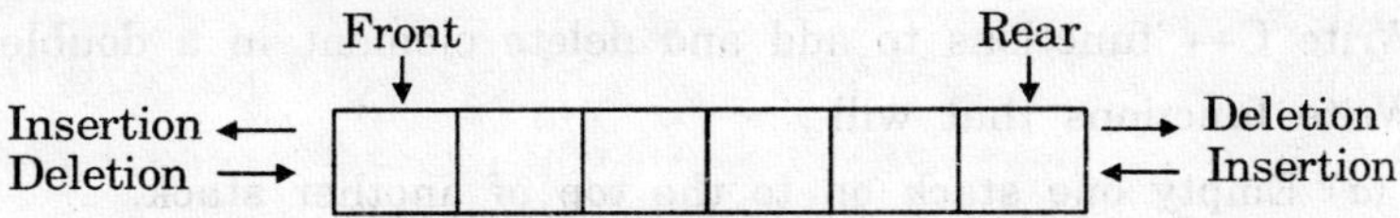

Fig. 3.9 De queue.

There are two different kinds of de queue, namely input restricted de queue and the output restricted de queue. The input restricted de queue allows insertions at only one end, while an output restricted de queue allows deletions from only one end.

3.2.4 Priority Queue

A queue, which we are able to insert items or remove items from any position based on the priority of the task to be processed, is called as a priority queue.

Fig. 3.10 represents a priority queue of customers waiting for a service. Priorities 1, 2 and 3 have been attached to customers, therefore the customers may get served according to their priority.

Customer Name	M	N	O	P	Q
Priority	3	5	1	4	2

Fig. 3.10 Priority queue

3.2.5 Applications of Queue

One of the area to which queues can be applied is that simulation. It is the process of forming an abstract model from a real situation in order to understand the impact of modifications and the effect of introducing various strategies on the situation.

During the process of a job the CPU following "first come first serve" scheduling strategy when there are more than one job. This strategy can be implemented in the data structure queue. When a program requests CPU time, it is placed at the back of the processor queue. The CPU currently serves the program at the head of the queue. When an executing program completes it is removed from the queue else it is placed at the back of process queue.

Another application of queue is traffic system where the queue is implemented when we frame the rules for average and maximum waiting time of the vehicles.

Exercises

1. Write C++ functions to implement a queue, which keeps the head of the queue always in the first position of linear array.
2. Write C++ functions to add and delete element in a circular queue.
3. Write C++ functions to add and delete element in a double-ended queue.
4. Write functions that will
   (*a*) Empty one stack on to the top of another stack.
   (*b*) Move all the items from a queue on to the stack.
5. What are stack frames for sub programs? What do they show?
6. Write a function that takes as input a C++ source code file and checks to make sure that the following symbols appear "balanced" in the source file: {}, /*, */, [], ().
7. Write a recursive procedure to solve Tower-of-Hanoi problem.

4

LINKED LIST

A Linked list is one of the fundamental data structures used in computer programming. It consists of a sequence of nodes, each containing arbitrary data fields and one or two references (links) pointing to the next and/or previous nodes. A linked list is called a self-referential data type because it contains a pointer or link to another data of the same type. Linked list permit insertion and removal of nodes at any point in the list but do not allow random access.

4.1 SINGLY LINKED LIST

The simplest kind of linked list is a singly linked list, which has one link per node. This link points to the next node in the list or to a null value or empty list if it is the last node.

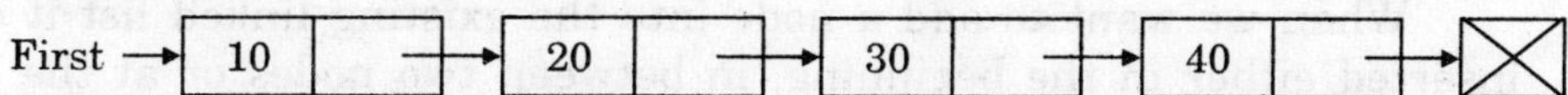

Fig. 4.1 A singly linked list containing 4 integer nodes

4.1.1. ADT of a Linked List

One node data structure will have two fields. We also keep an object head, which always points to the first node in the list.

```
class node
{
// object: a variable points to the first node of the list.
int data;
node* next;
public:
node *insert(int e);    //inserts item into linked list
node* delete(int e);  //deletes the given item
int search(int e);         // searches the item and returns its position
}
```

4.1.2 Representation of Linked List in C++

Creating an object called head of type node can form the linked list. Each node can have a link with another node by having the next node's address in its link field.

```
Class node
{
int data;
node* next;
public:
// operations
}
```

The above linked list can have only the integer data in it. The data type of the elements can be changed.

4.1.3 Linked List Operations

Traversal of a linked list is easy, beginning at the first node and following each next link until we come to an end.

```
temp = first;
While (temp! = null)
        temp = temp->next;
```

When we want to add a node into the existing linked list it can be inserted either in the beginning, in between two nodes or at the end of all the nodes.

The following figure represents how the node can be inserted at the beginning, which requires updating head.

```
newnode->next = first;
first = newnode;
```

Newnode represents the address of the node, which has to be inserted.

Newnode

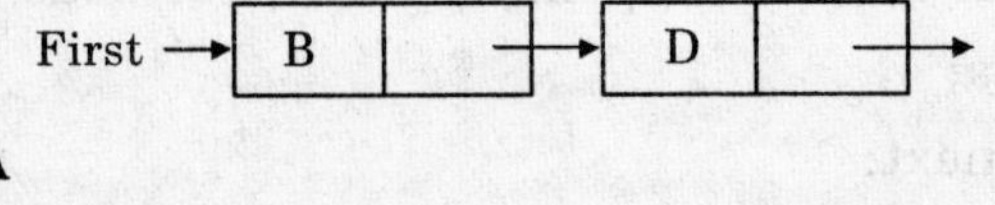

After adding A

First → A → B → D

The following code inserts a node after an existing node. The diagram shows how it works.

```
newnode->next = temp->next;
temp->next = newnode;
```

Temp is the address of the node after which the newnode has to be inserted.

Similarly we have functions for removing a node from the list. The diagram represents how the first node of the linked list can be deleted which affects the head node.

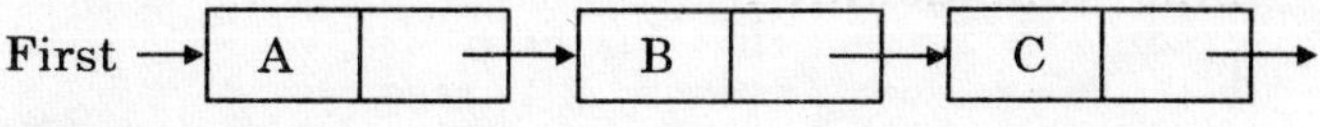

After deletion of A

First B C

The following code shows how the address of the head node can be changed.

```
temp = first;
first = first->next;
delete(temp);
```

When we want to delete the node, which is often a particular node, one must again keep track of the previous element.

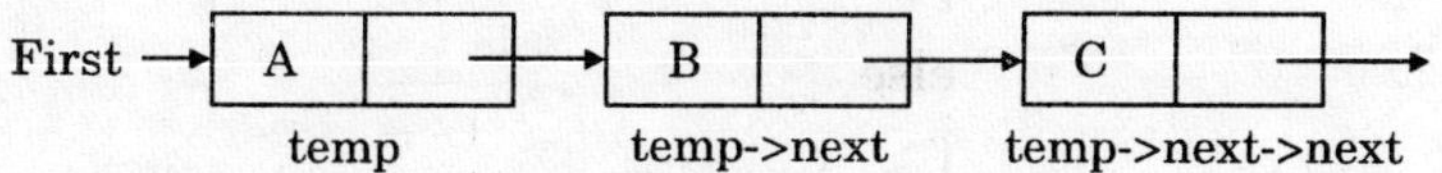

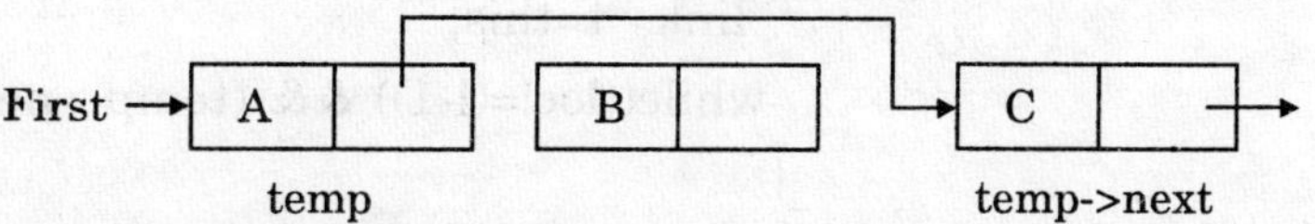

The removal code becomes

```
temp->next = temp->next->next;
```

Program to Add and Delete an Element in a Linear Linked List

```
#include<stdio.h>
#include<conio.h>
#include<iostream.h>
#define NULL 0
#include<process.h>
class link
{
    int data;
    link *next;
    public:
    link* add(int,int);
    link* del(int);
   void print();
```

```
};

link* link::del(int l)
{
    link *temp=this;
    if(this==NULL)
      cout<<"No";
    else
    {
        int loc=1;
         if(l==loc)
        {
            return(this->next);
        }
        else
        {
            link *temp = this;
            link *t=this;
            while((loc!=(l-1)) && (temp->next!=NULL))
            {
                temp=temp->next;
                loc++;
            }
            t=temp->next;
            temp->next=t->next;
            delete(t);
            return(this);
        }
    }
}
link* link::add(int d,int l)
{
    link *temp=this;
    link *newnode = new link;
     newnode->data = d;
    newnode->next=NULL;
     if (this == NULL)
```

```
    {
            return(newnode);
    }
      int loc=1;
     if (l==loc)
    {
            while(temp->next != NULL)
            temp = temp->next;
            temp->next=newnode;
            return(newnode);
     }
    else
    {
             while((loc!=(l-1)) && (temp->next!=NULL))
            {
                    temp=temp->next;
                    loc++;
            }
             newnode->next=temp->next;
             temp->next=newnode;
              return(this);
     }
  }
void link::print()
{
    if(this==NULL)
            cout<<"No node";
    else
    {
          link *p = this;
            do
          {
                cout<<p->data<<" ";
                p=p->next;
          }while(p!=NULL);
     }
}
```

```
void main()
{
    int c,c1;
    link *head;
    head=NULL;
    do
    {
        clrscr();
        cout<<"\t\tMenu\n";
        cout<<"\t1.Insert\n";
        cout<<"\t2.Delete\n";
        cout<<"\t3.Print\n";
        cout<<"\t4.Exit\n";
        cout<<"Enter your choice\n";
        cin>>c;
        int data,l;
        switch(c)
        {
            case 1:
            {
            cout<<"enter the data and location\n";
            cin>>data;
            cin>>l;
            head=head->add(data,l);
            break;
            }
            case 2:
            {
                cout<<"Enter the location \n";
                cin>>l;
                head=head->del(l);
                break;
            }
            case 3:
            {
                cout<<"node is \n";
                head->print();
```

```
                getch();
                break;
            }
            case 4:
            {
                exit(0);
            }
        }
    }while(c<=4);
    getch();
}
```

4.2 CIRCULAR LINKED LIST

Circular linked lists are more useful for describing naturally circular structures, and have the advantage of regular structure of being able to traverse the list starting at any point. They also allow quick access to the first and last records through a single pointer (the address of the last element). Their main disadvantage is the complexity of iteration, which has subtle special cases.

In circularly linked list, all nodes are linked in a continuous circle without using null pointer. The next node after the last node is the first node. It has the ability to traverse the full list beginning at any given node.

When we are inserting in an empty list the first node points itself.

```
first = newnode;
first->next = first;
```

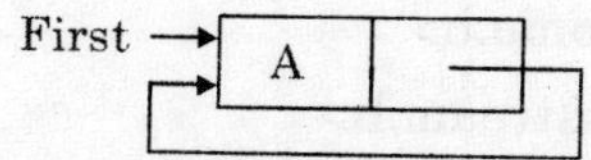

When we insert at the beginning of the node we need to change the last nodes next pointer also.

```
newnode->next  = first;
temp = first;
while(temp->next != first)
   temp = temp->next;
temp->next = newnode;
first = newnode;
```

First → B → C → D

Newnode

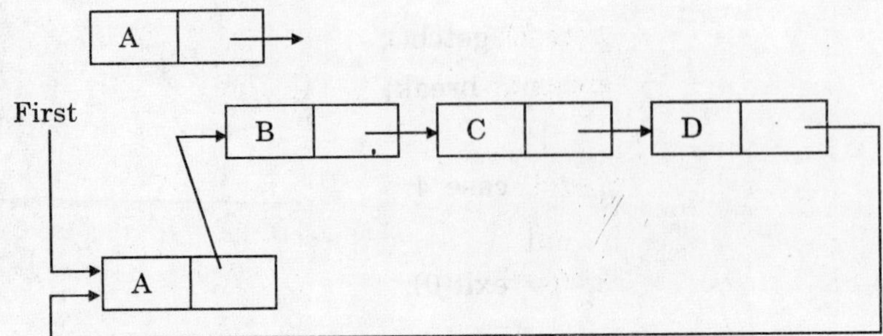

When we insert in between two nodes the code written in singly linked list can be followed. While deletion when we delete the first node we have to change last node pointer.

```
temp = first;
while(temp->next!= first)
temp->next = first->next;
temp->next = first->next;
first = first->next;
```

When we delete the last node, then the previous node must have the address of first node.

```
temp = first;
while (temp->next->next! = first)
temp = temp->next;
    temp->next = first;
```

The above code deletes the last node of circular linked list.

Program for Addition & Deletion of a Node Using Position in Circular Linked List

```
#include<stdio.h>
#include<conio.h>
#include<iostream.h>
#define NULL 0
#include<process.h>
class link
{
        int data;
        link *next;
        public:
        link* add(int,int);
        link* del(int);
        void print();
};
```

```
link* link::del(int l)
{
        link *temp=this;
        if(this==NULL)
                cout<<"No";
        else
        {
                int loc=1;
                if(l==loc)
                {
                        link *t=this;
                        while(temp->next!=this)
                                temp=temp->next;
                        temp->next=this->next;
                        delete(t);
                        return(this->next);
        }
        else
        {
        link *temp = this;
                        link *t=this;
                        while((loc!=(l-1)) && (temp->next!=this))
                        {
                                temp=temp->next;
                                loc++;
                        }
                        t=temp->next;
                        temp->next=t->next;
                        delete(t);
                        return(this);
                }
        }
}
link* link::add(int d,int l)
{
        link *temp=this;
        link *newnode = new link;
```

```
        newnode->data = d;
        if (this == NULL)
         {
              newnode->next=newnode;
              return(newnode);
        }
        int loc=1;
        if (l==loc)
        {
             newnode->next = this;
             while(temp->next != this)
                   temp = temp->next;
             temp->next=newnode;
             return(newnode);
          }
        else
       {
             while((loc!=(l-1)) && (temp->next!=this))
             {
                   temp=temp->next;
                   loc++;
             }
       newnode->next=temp->next;
       temp->next=newnode;
       return(this);
         }
    }
  void link::print()
 {
         if(this==NULL)
         cout<<"No node";
         else
         {
             link *p = this;
             do
              {
                   cout<<p->data<<" ";
```

```
                p=p->next;
            }while(p!=this);
        }
    }
void main()
{
    int c,c1;
    link *head;
    head=NULL;
    do
    {
        clrscr();
        cout<<"\t\tMenu\n";
        cout<<"\t1.Insert\n";
        cout<<"\t2.Delete\n";
        cout<<"\t3.Print\n";
        cout<<"\t4.Exit\n";
        cout<<"Enter your choice\n";
        cin>>c;
        int data,l;
        switch(c)
        {
            case 1:
            {
                cout<<"enter the data and location\n";
                cin>>data;
                cin>>l;
                head=head->add(data,l);
                break;
            }
            case 2:
            {
                cout<<"Enter the location \n";
                cin>>l;
                head=head->del(l);
                break;
            }
```

```
            case 3:
            {
                  cout<<"node is \n";
                  head->print();
                  getch();
                  break;
            }
            case 4:
            {
                  exit(0);
            }
      }
   }while(c<=4);
   getch();
}
```

4.3 DOUBLY LINKED LIST

A more sophisticated kind of linked list is a doubly linked list. Each node has two links one to the previous node and one to the next.

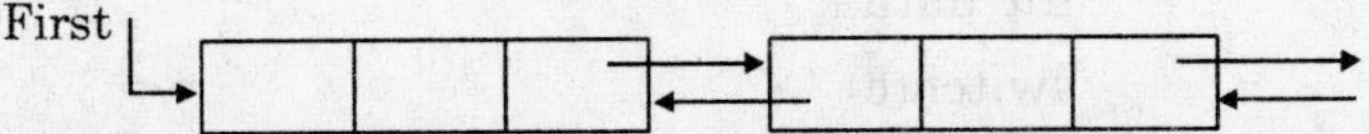

With double linked lists there are even more pointers to update, but less information is needed, since we can use backwards pointers to observe preceding elements in the list. We will add prev field to our node, pointing to the previous element. Iterating through a doubly linked list can be done in either direction.

```
Class node
{
node *prev;
int data;
node *next;
Public :
   // functions.
}
```

While adding a node to the front there is a change in first pointer. Which can be implemented as

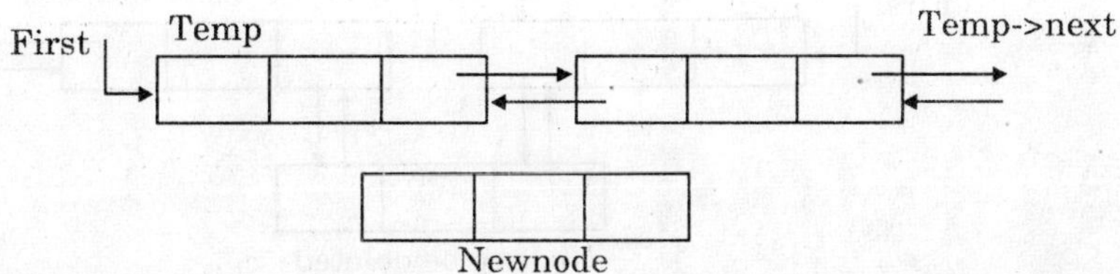

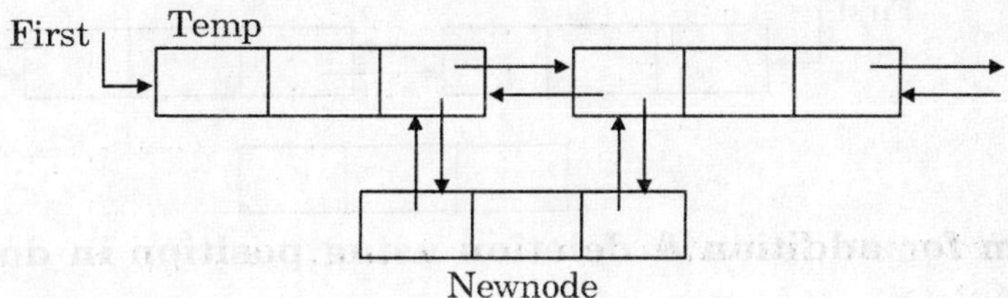


```
first->prev = newnode;
newnode->next = first;
newnode->prev=null;
first=newnode;
```

We also need a code to insert in between two nodes.

The following code insert the node in between two nodes of the doubly linked list and it is used for insertion at the end also.

```
newnode->next = temp->next;
temp->next->prev  = newnode;
newnode->prev = temp;
temp->next = newnode;
```

Removal of a node also can take place in the beginning, in between two nodes and at the end.

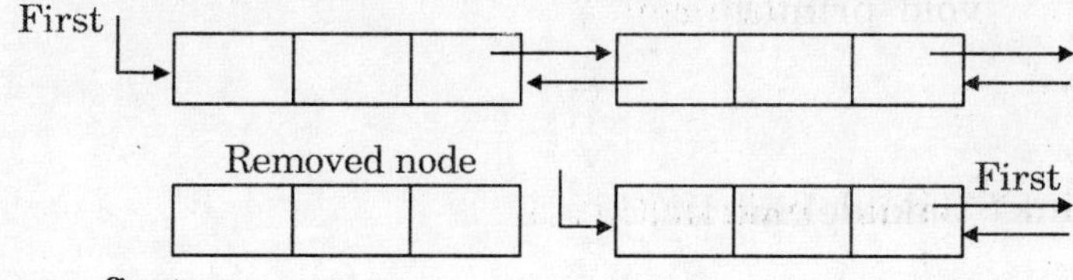


```
temp = first;
first->next->prev = null;
first = first->next;
delete(temp);
```

while deleting in between nodes, the nodes adjacent to the node to be deleted has to be taken care.

The following code can be used to delete the last node and in between nodes.

```
Temp->prev->next = temp->next;
Temp->next->prev = temp->prev;
```

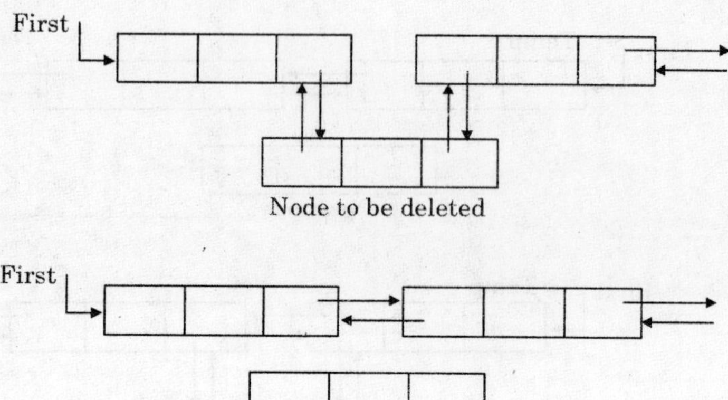

Program for addition & deletion using position in double linked list

```
#include<stdio.h>
#include<conio.h>
#include<iostream.h>
#define NULL 0
#include<process.h>
class link
{
    int data;
    link *rnext,*lnext;
    public:
     link* add(int,int);
    link* del(int);
    void print();
};

link* link::del(int l)
{
    link *temp=this;
    link *temp1=this;
    if(this==NULL)
        cout<<"No";
    else
    {
        int loc=1;
        if(l==loc)
        {
```

```
                    temp =this->rnext;
                    temp1=this;
                    delete(temp1);
                    temp->lnext=NULL;
                    return(temp);
                }
                else
                {
                    link *temp = this;
                    link *t=this;
                    while((loc!=(l-1)) && (temp->rnext!=NULL))
                    {
                        temp=temp->rnext;
                        loc++;
                    }
                    temp->lnext->rnext=temp->rnext;
                    temp->rnext->lnext=temp->lnext;
                    delete(temp);
                    return(this);
                }
        }
}
link* link::add(int d,int l)
{
        link *temp=this;
        link *newnode = new link;
        newnode->data = d;
        newnode->rnext=NULL;
        newnode->lnext=NULL;
        if (this == NULL)
        {
                return(newnode);
        }
        int loc=1;
        if (l==loc)
        {
                newnode->rnext = this;
```

```
                newnode->lnext=NULL;
                return(newnode);
        }
        else
        {
                while((loc!=(l-1)) && (temp->rnext!=NULL))
                {
                        temp=temp->rnext;
                        loc++;
                }
                newnode->rnext=temp->rnext;
                newnode->lnext=temp;
                temp->rnext->lnext=newnode;
                temp->rnext=newnode;
                return(this);
        }
    }
    void link::print()
    {
        if(this==NULL)
                cout<<"No node";
        else
        {
                 link *p = this;
                do
                {
                        cout<<p->data<<" ";
                        p=p->rnext;
                }while(p!=NULL);
        }
    }

  void main()
  {
        int c,c1;
        link *head;
        head=NULL;
        do
```

```
{
    clrscr();
    cout<<"\t\tMenu\n";
    cout<<"\t1.Insert\n";
    cout<<"\t2.Delete\n";
    cout<<"\t3.Print\n";
    cout<<"\t4.Exit\n";
    cout<<"Enter your choice\n";
    cin>>c;
    int data,l;
    switch(c)
    {
        case 1:
        {
            cout<<"enter the data and location\n";
            cin>>data;
            cin>>l;
            head=head->add(data,l);
            break;
        }
        case 2:
        {
            cout<<"Enter the location \n";
            cin>>l;
            head=head->del(l);
            break;
        }
        case 3:
        {
            cout<<"node is \n";
            head->print();
            getch();
            break;
        }
        case 4:
        {
            exit(0);
        }
```

```
        }
    }while(c<=4);
    getch();
}
```

4.4 APPLICATIONS OF LINKED LIST

Linked lists are used as building block for many other data structures, such as stacks, queues and their variations. The 'data' field of a node can be another linked list, so that we can construct many linked data structures with lists.

Some times, linked lists are used to implement associative arrays and are in the context called association lists. They are easily outperformed by other data structures such as self-balancing binary search trees even on small data sets. However, sometimes a linked list is dynamically created out of a subset of nodes in such a tree, and used more efficiently traverse that set.

Polynomial manipulations can be implemented by having a term of a polynomial in a node. Dictionary of names or any database can be implemented in a linked list.

4.4.1 Linked Stacks and Queues

We have already seen how to represent stacks and queues sequentially. When several stacks and queues co-exist, there is no efficient way to represent them sequentially. In this section we present a good solution to this problem using linked lists. The following figure shows a linked stack and a linked queue.

Linked Queue:

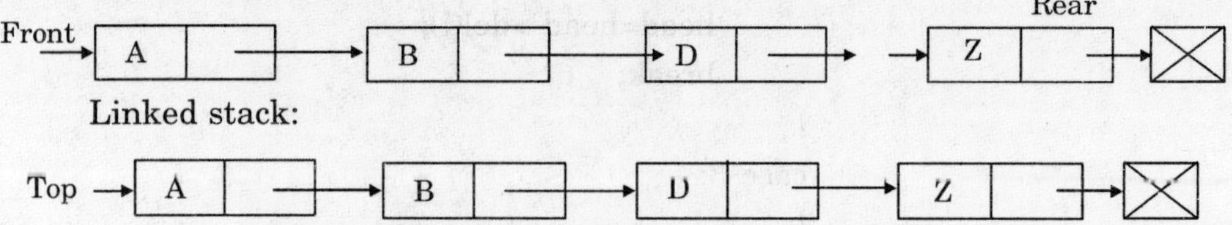

In a linked stack you can easily add and delete a node from top and in linked queue you can add a node at the rear and delete a node from front.

A collection of m stacks and n queues is obtained by the following:

```
Stack *s = new stack [m];
Queue *q = new queue [n];
```

Program for implementation of stack using linked list

```
#include<stdio.h>
#include<conio.h>
#include<iostream.h>
```

```
#define NULL 0
#include<process.h>
class link
{
        int data;
      link *next;
      public:
      link* push(int);
      link* pop();
      void print();
 };

link* link::pop()
{
      return(this->next);
 }
link* link::push(int d)
{
      link *newnode = new link;
      newnode->data = d;
      newnode->next = this;
      return(newnode);
  }
 void link::print()
 {
      link *p = this;
      While(p != NULL)
      {
            cout<<p->data<<" ";
            p=p->next;
      }
  }

void main()
{
      int c,c1;
      link *head;
```

```
head=NULL;
do
{
    clrscr();
    cout<<"\t\tMenu\n";
    cout<<"\t1.Insert\n";
    cout<<"\t2.Delete\n";
    cout<<"\t3.Print\n";
    cout<<"\t4.Exit\n";
    cout<<"Enter your choice\n";
    cin>>c;
    int data;
    switch(c)
    {
        case 1:
        {
            cout<<"enter the data\n";
            cin>>data;
            head=head->push(data);
            break;
        }
        case 2:
        {
            head=head->pop();
            break;
        }
        case 3:
        {
            cout<<"node is \n";
            head->print();
            getch();
            break;
        }
        case 4:
        {
            exit(0);
        }
```

```
                }
        }while(c<=5);
        getch();
    }
```

The following program shows the implementation of Queue in a Linked List.

Program for implementation of queue in linked list

```
#include<stdio.h>
#include<conio.h>
#include<iostream.h>
#define NULL 0
#include<process.h>
class link
{
        int data;
        link *next;
         public:
         link* insert(int);
        link* del();
         void print();
    };

link* link::del()
{
        return(this->next);
}

link* link::insert(int d)
{
        link *temp=this;
        link *newnode = new link;
        newnode->data = d;
        newnode->next = NULL;
        if (this == NULL)
                return(newnode);
        while(temp->next!=NULL)
                temp=temp->next;
```

```
            temp->next=newnode;
            return(this);
        }
        void link::print()
        {
            link *p = this;
            while(p != NULL)
            {
                cout<<p->data<<" ";
                p=p->next;
            }
        }

        void main()
        {
            int c,c1;
            link *head;
            head = NULL;
            do
            {
                clrscr();
                cout<<"\t\tMenu\n";
                cout<<"\t1.Insert\n";
                cout<<"\t2.Delete\n";
                cout<<"\t3.Print\n";
                cout<<"\t4.Exit\n";
                cout<<"Enter your choice\n";
                cin>>c;
                int data;
                switch(c)
                {
                    case 1:
                    {
                        cout<<"enter the data\n";
                        cin>>data;
                        head=head->insert(data);
                        break;
```

```
}
case 2:
{
      head=head->del();
      break;
}
case 3:
{
      cout<<"node is \n";
      head->print();
      getch();
      break;
}
case 4:
{
      exit(0);
}
    }
  }while(c<=4);
  getch();
}
```

Exercises

1. Write a function length which counts the number of nodes in a linked list. What is the time complexity of the algorithm?
2. Write a function to reverse the content of the singly linked list.
3. Write a function to remove the duplicate elements from a circular linked list.
4. When deleting an element from a linked stack or queue, we checked for emptiness, but when adding an item, we did not check for overflow. Why?
5. Implement queue in a circular linked list with one pointer rear.
6. Write a C++ program to add and delete an item from singly linked list by checking the value of the nodes in sorted order.
7. Write a function to sort the elements of doubly linked list in ascending order.
8. Write a function to concatenate two circular linked lists.
9. Write a function to make a doubly linked as circular.
10. Wiite a function to split a linear linked list.

5

TREES

Thus far we have been concerned with linear lists. The relationships that have been expressed by such data structures are essentially one-dimensional. In this chapter we will introduce data structures, which are non-linear and are, therefore, capable of expressing more complex relationships than that of physical adjacency.

5.1 DEFINITIONS AND CONCEPTS

We first consider the definition of a general graph and its associated terminology. A tree can be viewed as a restricted graph. The restriction imposed on a graph to define a tree yield a general tree. By considering the graphs given in fig. 5.1, we can define the graph.

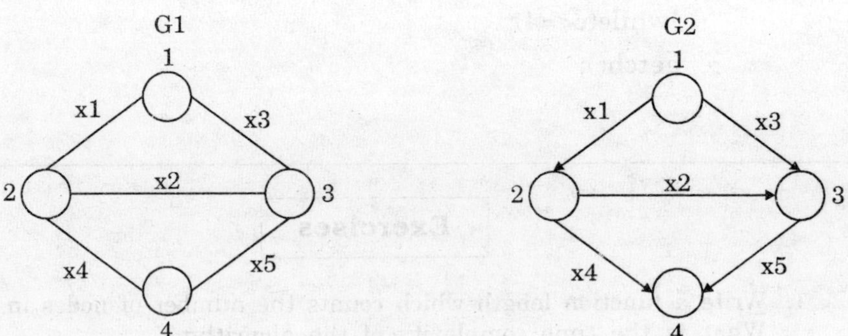

Fig. 5.1 Graph

A graph G consists of a non empty set V called the set of nodes (points, vertices) of the graph, a set E that is the set of edges of the graph, and a mapping from the set of edges E to a set of pairs of elements of V.

Any two nodes, which are connected by an edge in a graph, are called adjacent nodes. For example, in G1 the nodes 1 and 2 are adjacent to each other.

In a graph G = (V, E) an edge which is directed from one node to another is called directed edge. While an edge, which has, no specific direction is called an undirected edge. A graph in which every edge is undirected is called an undirected graph. A graph in which every edge is directed is called a directed graph or digraph. In fig. 5.1 G1 is called as undirected graph and G2 is called as digraph.

An edge of a graph which joins a node to itself is a called a loop. We may have certain pairs of nodes joined by more than one edge. Such edges are called parallel. In fig. 5.2 there are three parallel edges joining the nodes 1 and 2, two parallel edges joining nodes 2 and 3 and a loop in 3. Any graph, which contains some parallel edges, is called a multi graph.

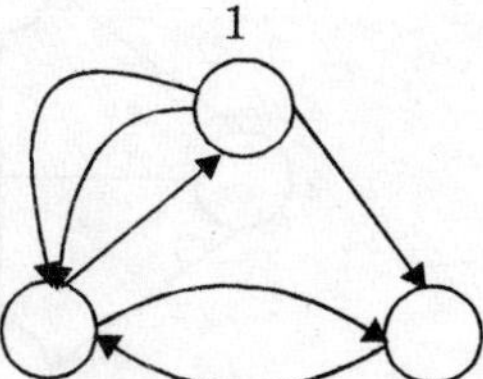

Fig. 5.2 Multi graph

A graph in which weights are assigned to every node is called a weighted graph. For example, a graph of city streets may be assigned weights according to the distance between two streets.

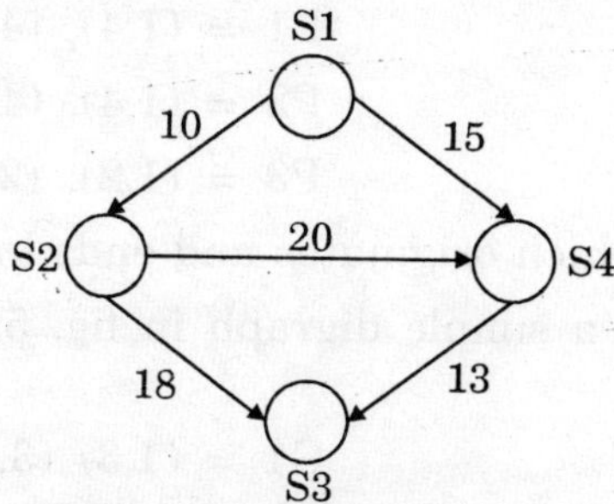

Fig. 5.3 Weighted graph

In a graph a node, which is not adjacent to any other node, is called an isolated node. A graph containing only isolated nodes is called a null graph. Fig. 5.4 (a) has an isolated node and fig. 5.4 (b) is a null graph.

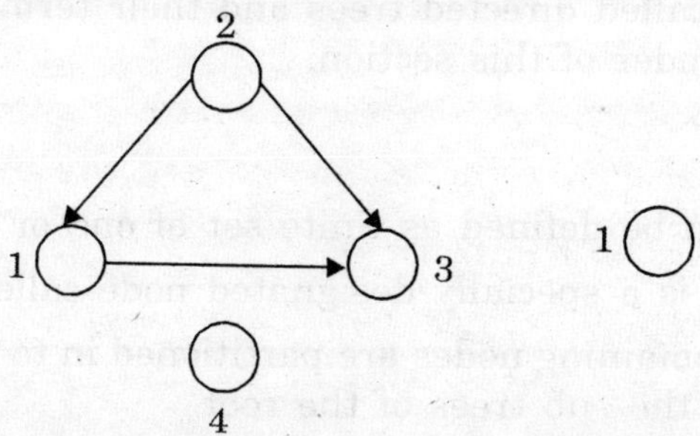

Fig. 5.4 (a) Isolated node graph (b) Null graph

In a directed graph for any node V the number of edges, which have V as their initial node is called the out degree of the node V the number of edges, which have V as their terminal node is called the in degree of V.

In a directed graph given in fig. 5.5, consider the vertex 2, the in degree of node 2 is 3, and out degree of node 2 is 1. Any sequence of edges of a digraph such that the terminal node of any edge in the sequence is the initial node of the edge, if any, appearing next in the sequence defines a path of the graph. The number of edges appearing in the sequence of the path is called the length of the path.

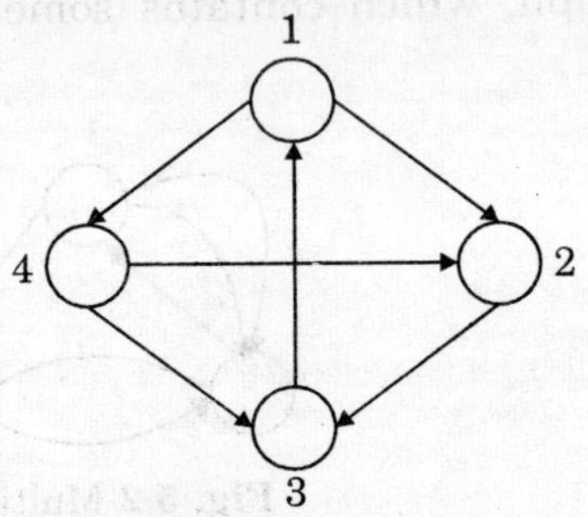

Fig. 5.5 Digraph

Consider a digraph given in fig. 5.5 some of the paths starting from node 1 and ending in node 3 are

P1 = (1,4), (4,3)

P2 = (1,4), (4,2), (2,3)

P3 = (1,2), (2,3)

A path which originates and ends in the same node is called a cycle.

Consider a simple digraph in fig. 5.5. Some of the cycles are given as follows.

C1 = (1,3) (3,1)

C2 = (1,4) (4,3) (3,1)

C3 = (1,2) (2,3) (3,1)

A simple digraph, which does not have any cycle, is called a cyclic. Naturally such graphs cannot have any loops. An important class of digraphs called directed trees and their terminology will be discussed in the remainder of this section.

5.2 TREES

A tree can be defined as finite set of one or more nodes such that:

(1) There is a specially designated node called as the root.

(2) The remaining nodes are partitioned in to $n \geq 0$ disjoint sets $T_1..T_n$ are called the sub trees of the root.

There are many terms that are often used when referring to trees. A node stands for the item of information plus the branches to other nodes. Consider the tree in fig. 5.6. This tree has 15 nodes.

The number of sub trees of a node is called its degree. The degree of A and G is 3, of B, D and E is 2, of G and I is 1. Nodes that have degree zero are called leaf or terminal nodes. F, H, K, K, L, M, N, and O are called leaf nodes. Children of the same parent are said to be siblings. B, C, and D are siblings. The ancestors of a node are all the nodes along the path from the root to that node. The ancestors of J are A, B and E.

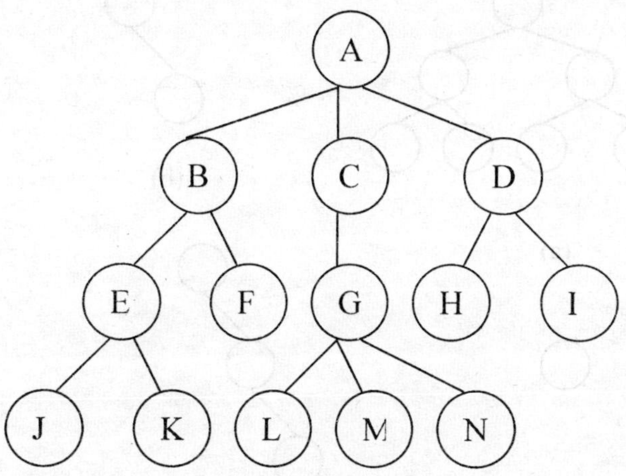

Fig. 5.6 Tree

The level of a node is defined by letting the root is at level one. If a node is at level L, then its children are at level L + 1. The height or depth of a tree is defined to be the maximum level of any node in the tree.

5.3 BINARY TREE

Binary tree can be defined as a finite set of nodes that either is empty or consists of a root and two disjoint binary trees called the left sub tree and right sub tree.

Binary trees are categorized by the fact that any node can have at most two branches. Also a binary tree may have zero nodes.

5.3.1 ADT of a Binary Tree

ADT defines the set of operations on binary trees. Fig. 5.7 shows some of the binary trees.

```
Class treenode
{
//object: finite set of nodes either empty or consisting of root node, left
//sub tree and right sub tree.
Public:
    treenode(); //creates node
    boolean isempty(); //returns true when tree is empty
```

```
treenode* create(treenode *t1, int item, treenode *t2); //create a
node with item
    treenode lchild(); //returns left sub tree of *this
    treenode rchild(); //returns right sub tree of *this
}
```

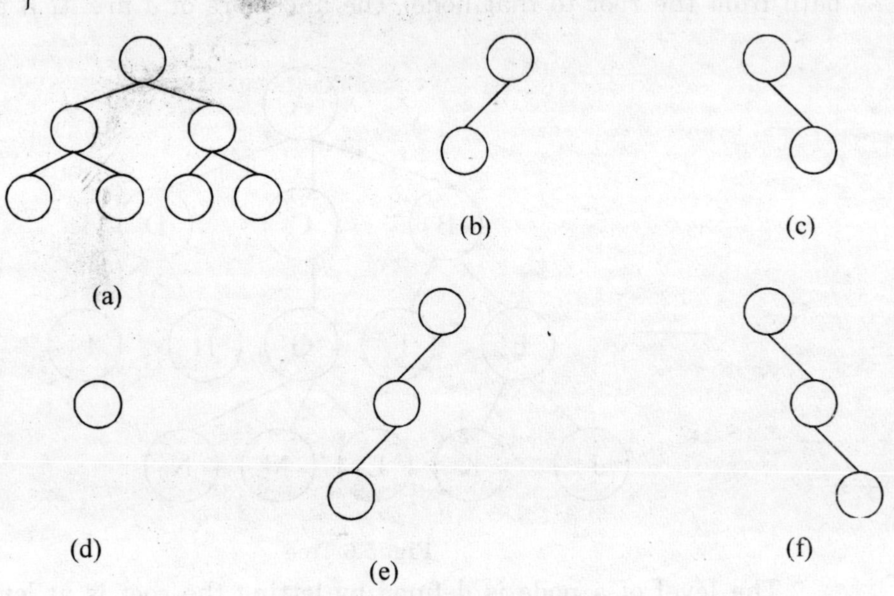

Fig. 5.7 Binary trees

Figs. 5.7 (*e*) and (*f*) shows two special kinds of binary trees. The tree in fig. 5.7(*e*) is a skewed tree, skewed to the left and there is a corresponding tree that skews to the right given in fig. 5.7 (*f*). The tree in fig. 5.7 (*a*) is called complete binary tree.

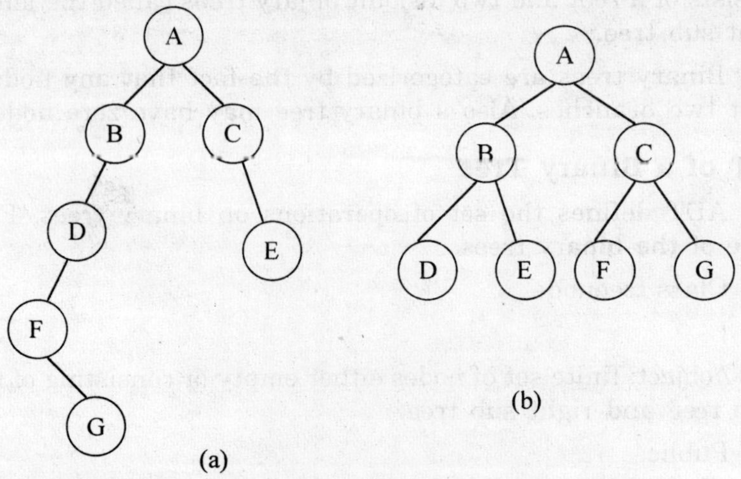

5.3.2 Binary Tree Representation

Consider the tree in fig. 5.8, we can use one-dimensional array to store the nodes. To find the locations of left, right and parent of any node we can use the following rules.

If a complete binary tree with n nodes is represented sequentially, then for any node with index i, we have:

1. Parent(i) is at [i/2] if $i \neq 1$. If $i = 1$, i is at the root and has no parent.
2. Left child(i) is at 2i if $2i \leq n$. If $2i > n$ then i has no left child.
3. Right child(i) is at $2i + 1$ if $2i + 1 \leq n$. If $2i + 1 > n$ then i has no right child.

Index	(c)
[0]	
[1]	A
[2]	B
[3]	C
[4]	D
[5]	
[6]	
[7]	E
[8]	F
[9]	
[10]	
[11]	
[12]	
[13]	
[14]	
[15]	
[16]	
[17]	G

(c)

Index	(d)
[0]	
[1]	A
[2]	B
[3]	C
[4]	D
[5]	E
[6]	F
[7]	G
[8]	
[9]	
[10]	
[11]	
[12]	
[13]	
[14]	
[15]	
[16]	
[17]	

(d)

Fig. 5.8 Binary tree array representation

This representation can be used for all binary trees, though in most cases there will be a lot of unused spaces. Fig. 5.8 shows the array representation of both the trees. But in fig. 5.8 (c) there is lot of unused spaces. Since fig. 5.8 (b) is a complete binary tree it uses the array efficiently.

5.3.3 Linked Representation

Even though the array representation of a binary tree is quite easier, it is wasteful for many other binary trees. Insertion and deletion of nodes from the middle of the tree require movement of many nodes. These problems can be overcome through the use of linked representation. Such a tree having the nodes of the form shown in fig. 5.9, where Lchild and

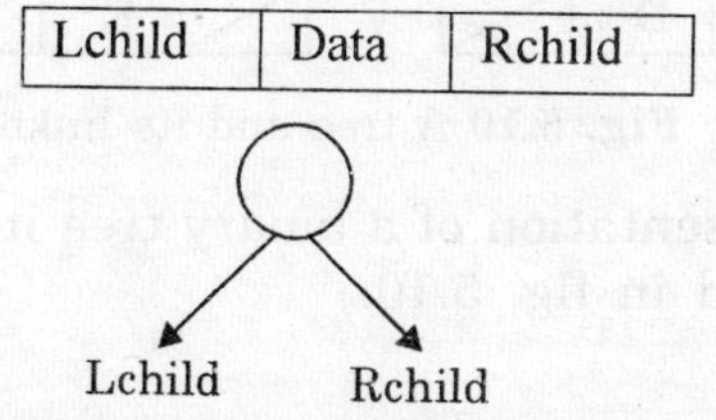

Fig. 5.9 Binary tree node representation

R-child denote the addresses of left and right sub trees respectively of a particular node. Empty sub trees are represented by a pointer value of NULL. DATA specifies the information associated with a node.

We will use two classes to implement the above node in a tree.

```
Class tree;        //forward declaration
Class treenode
{
friend class tree;
private:
    treenode *lchild;
    treenode *rchild;
};
class tree
{
private:
    treenode *root;
public:
    //tree operations
}
```

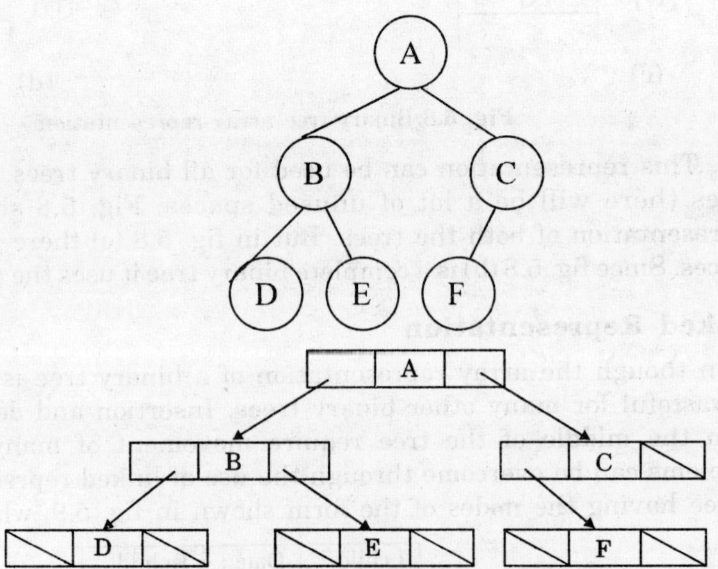

Fig. 5.10 A tree and its linked representation

The representation of a binary tree in the linked representation has been structured in fig. 5.10.

5.4 BINARY TREE TRAVERSAL

One of the most common operations performed on tree structures is that of traversal. This is the procedure by which each node in the tree is processed exactly once in a systematic manner. The meaning of processed depends on the nature of the application.

When traversing a binary tree, we want to treat each node and its sub trees in the same fashion. If we let L, V and R standing for moving left, visiting the node and moving right, then there are six possible combinations of traversal: LVR, LRV, VLR, VRL, RVL and RLV. If we consider the traversals left before right then only three traversals remain: LVR, LRV and VLR. To these we assign the names inorder, postorder and preorder, respectively.

There is a natural correspondence between these traversals and producing infix, postfix and prefix forms of expression.

5.4.1 Inorder Traversal

The inorder traversal of a binary tree is defined as follows.

1. Traverse the left subtree in inorder.
2. Process the root node.
3. Traverse the right sub tree in inorder.

Consider the binary tree in fig. 5.11. The inorder traversal of the tree results the following sequence.

a+b*c–d

This is the infix form of the expression.

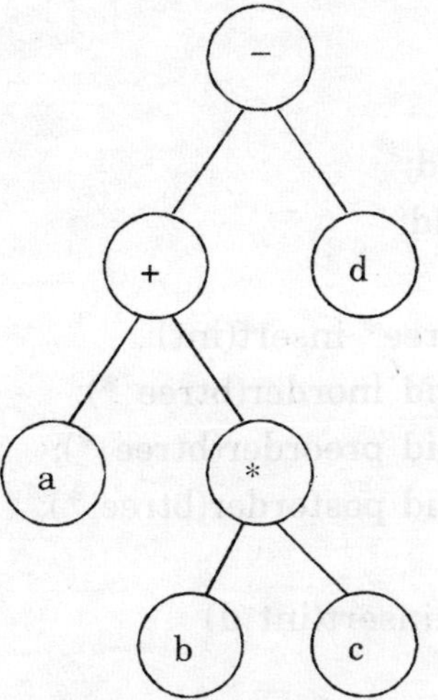

Fig. 5.11 Binary tree

5.4.2 Preorder Traversal

The following steps give the preorder traversal of a binary tree.

1. Process the root node.
2. Traverse the left sub tree in preorder.
3. Traverse the right sub tree in preorder.

If a particular sub tree is empty doing nothing performs the traversal. The preorder traversal of the tree in fig. 5.11 gives the following processing order.

–+a*bcd

5.4.3 Postorder Traversal

We define the postorder traversal of a binary tree as follows:

1. Traverse the left sub tree in postorder.
2. Traverse the right sub tree in postorder.
3. Process the root node.

The postorder traversal of the tree in fig. 5.11 gives the following processing order.

abc*+d–

The C++ implementations of above traversal algorithms are given in the following program.

Program for binary tree traversal (Recursion) method

```
#include<iostream.h>
#include<conio.h>
#include<stdio.h>
#include<process.h>
class btree
 {
  int data;
  btree *lchild;
  btree *rchild;
  public:
            btree* insert(int);
            void inorder(btree *);
            void preorder(btree *);
            void postorder(btree *);
 };
btree* btree::insert(int d)
 {
            int flag;
            btree *newnode = new btree;
            newnode->data=d;
            newnode->lchild = NULL;
```

```
				newnode->rchild = NULL;
				if(this == NULL)
					return (newnode);
				else
				{
					btree *temp=this;
					btree *prev=this;
					while(temp != NULL)
					{
						if(d<temp->data)
						{
							prev = temp;
							temp = temp->lchild;
							flag = 0;
						}
						else
						{
							prev = temp;
							temp = temp->rchild;
							flag = 1;
						}
					}
				if(flag == 0)
				{
					prev->lchild = newnode;
				}
				else
				{
					prev->rchild = newnode;
				}
				return(this);
			}
		}
	void btree::inorder(btree *currentnode)
	{
		if(currentnode != NULL)
		{
			inorder(currentnode->lchild);
			cout<<currentnode->data<<" ";
			inorder(currentnode->rchild);
```

```
        }
    }
void btree::preorder(btree *currentnode)
    {
        if(currentnode !=NULL)
        {
            cout<<currentnode->data<<" ";
            preorder(currentnode->lchild);
            preorder(currentnode->rchild);
        }
    }
void btree::postorder(btree *currentnode)
    {
        if(currentnode !=NULL)
        {
            postorder(currentnode->lchild);
            postorder(currentnode->rchild);
            cout<<currentnode->data<<" ";
        }
    }
void main()
    {
        btree *tree = NULL;
        clrscr();
        int d,c;
        do
        {
        clrscr();
        cout<<"\t\tProgram For Binary Tree\n";
        cout<<"\t1.Create\n";
        cout<<"\t2.Inorder\n";
        cout<<"\t3.Preorder\n";
        cout<<"\t4.Postorder\n";
        cout<<"\t5.Exit\n";
        cout<<"Enter your choice\n";
        cin>>c;
        switch(c)
```

```
{
        case 1:
            {
                cout<<"Enter the element\n";
                cin>>d;
                tree = tree->insert(d);
                break;
            }
        case 2:
            {
                cout<<"Printing Inorder Form\n";
                tree->inorder(tree);
                getch();
                break;
            }
        case 3:
            {
                cout<<"Printing Preorder Form\n";
                tree->preorder(tree);
                getch();
                break;
            }
        case 4:
            {
                cout<<"Printing Postorder Form\n";
                tree->postorder(tree);
                getch();
                break;
            }
        case 5:
            {
                exit(0);
            }
    }
    }while(c<=5);
}
```

5.5 THREADED STORAGE REPRESENTATION OF BINARY TREES

The wasted NULL links in the storage representation of binary trees can be replaced by threads. A binary tree is threaded according to a particular traversal order. For example, the threads for the inorder traversal of a tree are pointers to its higher nodes. For this traversal order, if the left link of a node P is normally NULL, then this link is replaced by the address of the predecessor of P. Similarly a NULL right link is replaced by the address of successor of P.

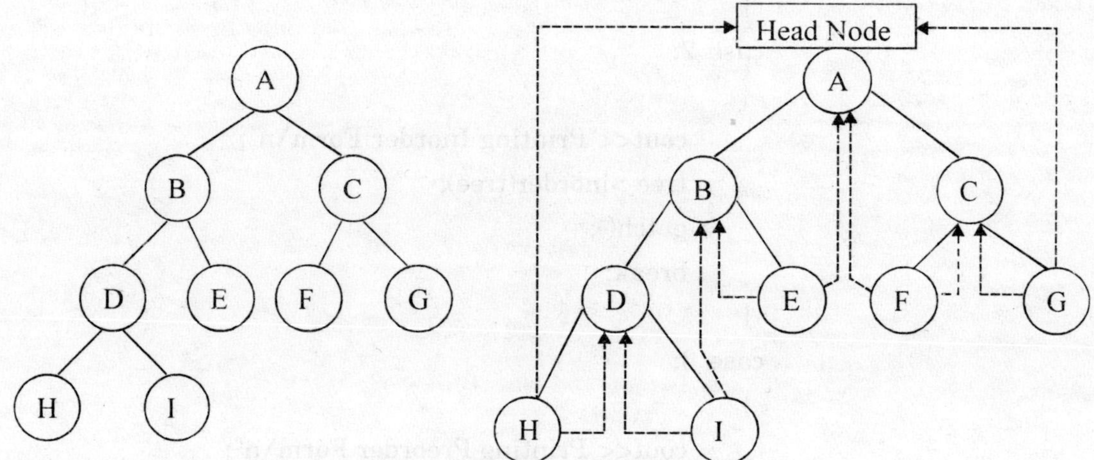

Fig. 5.12 Threaded binary tree

Fig. 5.12 shows the binary tree and its new form with threads drawn as broken lines.

There is a node called head node, which serves as the predecessor and successor of the first and last tree nodes with respect to inorder traversal. Threaded binary tree will have a circular form with its head node.

Lchild	Lthread	Data	Rthread	Rchild

Fig. 5.13 A node of a threaded binary tree

In memory representation we must be able to distinguish between thread and structural pointers. Adding two Boolean fields Lthread and Rthread does this. The following coding scheme is used to distinguish between structural link and a thread, which is shown in fig. 5.13.

Lthread = True denotes left thread link.

Lthread = False denotes left structural link.

Rthread = True denotes right thread link.

Rthread = False denotes right structural link.

The complete representation can be given by implementing the structure of thread node, which is shown in fig. 5.13 in to a threaded tree shown in fig. 5.12.

5.6 BINARY SEARCH TREE

When we want to perform the functions like search, insert and delete, binary search tree's performance is better than any other data structures.

A binary search tree is a binary tree, which satisfies the following properties:

- Every element has a key and no two elements have the same key.
- The keys in the left sub tree are smaller than the key in the root.
- The keys in the right sub tree are greater than the key in the root.
- The left and right sub trees are also binary sub trees.

Example of a binary search tree is shown in fig. 5.14.

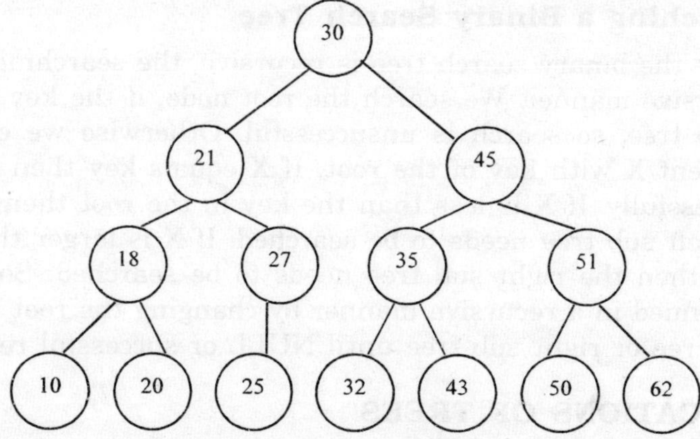

Fig. 5.14 Binary search tree

5.6.1 Insertion

Insertion begins with a search; we search for the value, but if we do not find it, we search the left or right subtrees as before. Eventually, we will reach an external node, and we add the value at that position. In other words, we examine the root and recursively insert the new node to the left subtree if the new value is less than or equal the root, or the right subtree if the new value is greater than the root.

5.6.2 Deletion

There are several cases to consider:

- Deleting a leaf: Deleting a node with no children is easy, as we can simply remove it from the tree.
- Deleting a node with one child: Delete it and replace it with its child.
- Deleting a node with two children: Suppose the node to be deleted is called N. We replace the value of N with either its in-order successor

(the left-most child of the right subtree) or the in-order predecessor (the right-most child of the left subtree).

Once we find either the in-order successor or predecessor, swap it with N, and then delete it. Since either of these nodes must have less than two children (otherwise it cannot be the in-order successor or predecessor), it can be deleted using the previous two cases.

In a good implementation, it is generally recommended to avoid consistently using one of these nodes, because this can unbalance the tree.

5.6.3 Traversal

Once the binary search tree has been created, its elements can be retrieved in inorder by recursively traversing the left subtree, visiting the root, then recursively traversing the right subtree. The tree may also be traversed in preorder and postorder traversals.

5.6.4 Searching a Binary Search Tree

Since the binary search tree is recursive, the searching can be done in a recursive manner. We search the root node, if the key is zero then there is no tree, so search is unsuccessful. Otherwise we compare searching element X with key of the root. If X equals key then search terminates successfully. If X is less than the key in the root then only the nodes in the left sub tree needs to be searched. If X is larger than the key in the root then the right sub tree needs to be searched. So searching can be continued in a recursive manner by changing the root node as either left sub tree or right sub tree until NULL or successful result.

5.7 APPLICATIONS OF TREES

Mechanical manipulation of arithmetic expression can be done by representing it as binary tree. The value of the expression can be evaluated by implementing a recursive algorithm on a binary tree.

An interesting application of tree is concerning the construction and maintenance of symbol table. The two required operations that must be performed on a symbol table are insertion and look up, each of which involves searching. Since symbol table is implemented in a tree structure the table searching becomes approximately equivalent to a binary search.

The tree also plays an important role in the area of syntax analysis, where it is used to display the structure of sentence in a language and is used in defining unambiguous languages.

Exercises

1. Construct all possible binary trees with 4 nodes.
2. Draw a binary tree for the expression

   A + B*C^D – (E + F)/G.
3. Write a function that will find the height of a linked binary tree.
4. Write a function that will count the leaves of a linked binary tree.
5. Draw a binary search tree that is formed by inserting data elements with key values A, Z, B, Y, C, X, D, W, E, and F in the order given.
6. Write a C++ program to traverse the binary tree in non-recursive manner.
7. Prove that an inorder traversal of a binary search tree visits the data elements stored in the tree in sorted order.
8. How can threads be distinguished from other pointers in the binary tree?
9. What advantages do threaded trees offer?
10. Write a function getsize() which returns the size of a binary tree.

6

GRAPH

In the last chapter itself we have discussed about graph, node, edge, path, cycle, etc. This section is concerned with a further discussion of graphs and their representations.

6.1 GRAPH REPRESENTATION

There are three different ways of representing a graph. They are adjacency matrices, adjacency lists and adjacency multi lists. The choice of a representation will depend upon the application.

6.1.1 Adjacency Matrix

Given a simple digraph G = (V, E). A matrix representation of G depends upon the ordering of the nodes.

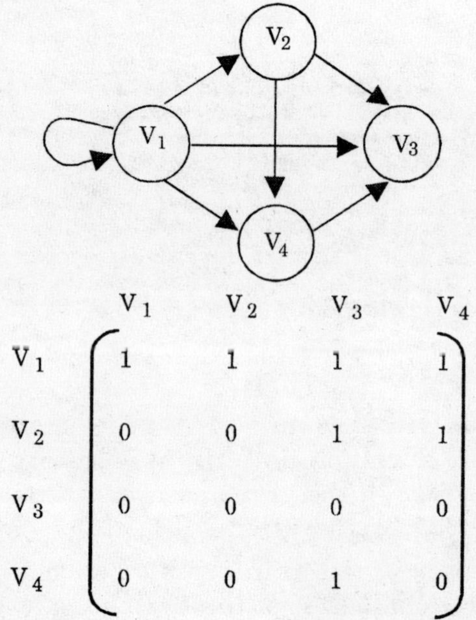

Fig. 6.1 A digraph and its adjacency matrix

Let G = (V, E) be a simple digraph in which $V = (V_1, V_2, V_3 \ldots V_n)$ and the nodes are assumed to be ordered from V_1 to V_n. An n*n matrix A whose elements a_{ij} are given by

$a_{ij} = 1$ if $(V_i, V_j) \varepsilon E$

is called the adjacency matrix of the Graph G.

Consider a digraph given in fig. 6.1 in which the order of the nodes is given as V_1, V_2, V_3 and V_4. The adjacency matrix is given in fig. 6.1.

6.1.2 Adjacency List Representation

In this representation, the n rows of the adjacency matrix are represented as linked lists. There is one list for each vertex in G. The nodes in list I represent the vertices that are adjacent from vertex i. Each node has at least two field's data and link. The adjacency list for graph given in fig. 6.1 is shown in fig. 6.2.

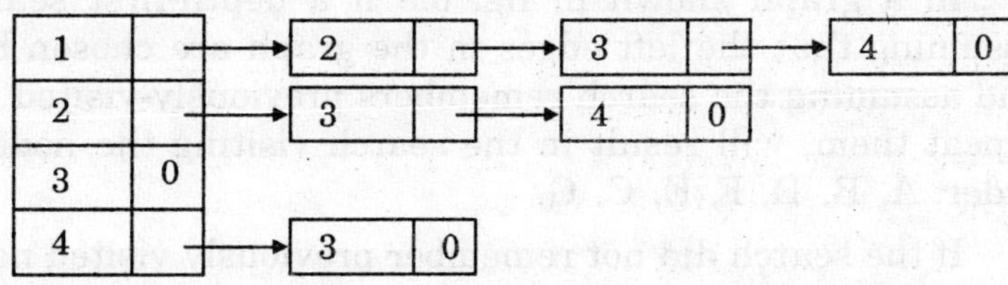

Fig. 6.2 Adjacency list

6.1.3 Adjacency Multi List

In the adjacency multi list representation, each edge (u,v) is represented by two entries, one on the list of u and other on the list of v. the node structure is

m	Vertex 1	Vertex 2	List 1	List 2

Where m is a boolean mark field that may be used to indicate whether or not the edge has been examined.

6.2 DEPTH FIRST SEARCH

Depth-First Search (DFS) is an algorithm for traversing or searching a tree, tree structure, or graph. Intuitively, you start at the root (selecting some node as the root in the graph case) and explore as far as possible along each branch before backtracking.

Formally, DFS is an uninformed search that progresses by expanding the first child node of the search tree that appears and thus going deeper and deeper until a goal state is found, or it hits a node that has no children. Then the search backtracks and starts off on the next node.

All freshly expanded nodes are added to a LIFO stack for expansion.

Space complexity of DFS is much lower compared to BFS (Breadth-First Search). It also lends itself much better to heuristic methods of choosing a likely-looking branch.

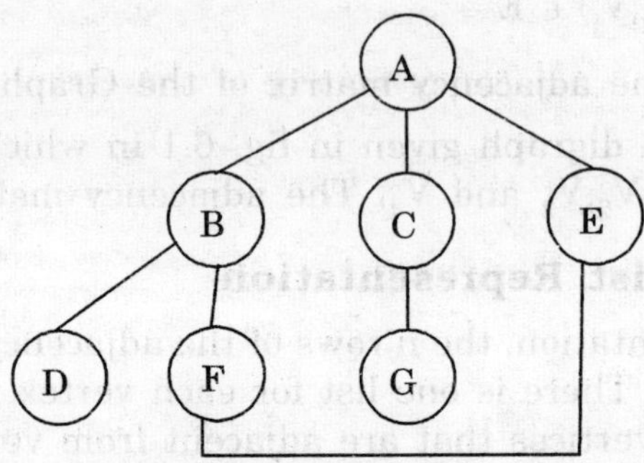

Fig. 6.3. Graph

In a graph shown in fig. 6.3 if a depth-first search starting at A, assuming that the left edges in the graph are chosen before right edges, and assuming the search remembers previously-visited nodes and will not repeat them, will result in the search visiting the nodes in the following order: A, B, D, F, E, C, G.

If the search did not remember previously visited nodes, but given the other conditions in the previous paragraph, the search would proceed as A, B, D, F, E, A, B, D, F, E, etc. forever, caught in the A, B, D, F, E cycle and never reaching C or G.

Iterative deepening prevents this loop and will reach the following nodes on the following depths, assuming it proceeds left-to-right as above:

- 0: A
- 1: A (repeated), B, C, E

(Note that iterative deepening has now seen C, when a conventional depth-first search did not.)

- 2: A, B, D, F, C, G, E, F

(Note that it still sees C, but that it came later. Also note that it sees E via a different path, and loops back to F twice.)

- 3: A, B, D, F, E, C, G, E, F, B

For this graph, as more depth is added, the two cycles "ABFE" and "AEFB" will simply get longer before the algorithm gives up and tries another branch.

Program for graph traversal depth first algorithm

```
#include<iostream.h>
#include<stdio.h>
#include<conio.h>
class gra
```

```
    {
      int ad[20][20];
      int size;
      int *visited;
      public:
            gra(int s)
            {
            size = s;
            visited = new int[s];
            }
            void get();
            void dfs(int);
    };
  void gra::get()
    {
            int a1;
            cout<<"Enter the relation\n";
            for(int i=1;i<=size;i++)
            {
                  for(int j=1;j<=size;j++)
                  {
                        cout<<"Enter "<<i<<" "<<j<<" "<<"Relation"<<endl;
                        cin>>a1;
                        if(a1==1)
                              ad[i][j]=1;
                        else
                              ad[i][j]=0;
            }
      }
      for(i=1;i<=size;i++)
            visited[i]=0;
      cout<<"1";
      dfs(1);
    }

  void gra::dfs(int v)
    {
```

```
    visited[v]=1;
    for(int j=1;j<=size;j++)
     {
         if(ad[v][j]!=0)
         {
              if(visited[j]==0)
              {
                   visited[j]=1;
                  cout<<j<<" ";
                  dfs(j);
              }
         }
     }
}

void main()
 {
      clrscr();
      cout<<"Enter the no of node\n";
      int c;
      cin>>c;
      gra G(c);
      G.get();
      getch();
 }
```

6.3 BREADTH-FIRST SEARCH

In computer science, Breadth-First Search (BFS) is a tree search algorithm used for traversing or searching a tree, tree structure, or graph. Intuitively, you start at the root node and explore all the neighboring nodes. Then for each of those nearest nodes, explore their unexplored neighbor nodes, and so on until it finds the goal.

Formally, BFS is an uninformed search method that aims to expand and examine all nodes of a tree systematically in search of a solution. In other words, it exhaustively searches the entire tree without considering the goal until it finds it. It does not use a heuristic.

From the standpoint of the algorithm, all child nodes obtained by expanding a node are added to a FIFO queue. In typical implementations, nodes that have not yet been examined for their neighbors are placed in some container (such as a queue or linked list) called "open" and then once examined are placed in the container "closed".

When searching in an unweighted cyclic graph for a shortest path, BFS may be adapted by keeping a bit on each node to indicate that it has already been visited.

Consider a graph in fig. 6.3, breadth-first search starting at A, and assuming that the left edges in the shown graph are chosen before right edges, will result in the search visiting the nodes in the following order: A, B, C, E, D, F, G.

Program for graph traversal using breadth first algorithm

```
#include<iostream.h>
#include<stdio.h>
#include<conio.h>
class gra
{
  int ad[20][20];
  int size;
  int visited[20];
  public:
        gra(int s){size=s;}
        void get();
        void bfs(int);
};
void gra::get()
{
        int a1,i,j;
        cout<<"Enter the relation\n";
        for(i=1;i<=size;i++)
        {
                for(j=1;j<=size;j++)
                {
                        cout<<"Enter "<<i<<" "<<j<<" "<<"Relation"<<endl;
                        cin>>a1;
                        if(a1==1)
                                ad[i][j]=1;
                        else
                                ad[i][j]=0;
                }
```

```
    }
    cout<<"\nAd. Matrix is :\n";
    for(i=1;i<=size;i++)
    {
        for(j=1;j<=size;j++)
        {
            cout<<ad[i][j]<<" ";
        }
        cout<<endl;
    }
    cout<<endl;
}

void gra::bfs(int v)
{
    for(int i=1;i<=size;i++)
        visited[i]=0;
    visited[v]=1;
    cout<<v<<" ";
    int q[10];
    int rear,front;
    ear=front=0;
    q[rear]=v;
    rear++;
    while(rear!=front)
    {
        v=q[front];
        front++;
        for(int j=1;j<=size;j++)
        {
            if(ad[v][j]!=0)
            {
                if(visited[j]==0)
                {
                    q[rear]=j;
                    rear++;
                    visited[j]=1;
```

```
                    cout<<j<<" ";
                }
            }
        }
    }
}

void main()
  {
    clrscr();
    cout<<"Enter the no of node\n";
    int c;
    cin>>c;
    gra G(c);
    G.get();
    cout<<"Breadth First Algorithm of Given Graph\n";
    G.bfs(1);
    getch();
  }
```

6.4 SPANNING TREE

Given a connected, undirected graph, a spanning tree of that graph is a subgraph which is a tree and connects all the vertices together. A single graph can have many different spanning trees. We can also assign a weight to each edge, which is a number representing how unfavorable it is, and use this to assign a weight to a spanning tree by computing the sum of the weights of the edges in that spanning tree. A minimum spanning tree or minimum weight spanning tree is then a spanning tree with weight less than or equal to the weight of every other spanning tree. More generally, any undirected graph has a minimum spanning forest. Fig. 6.4 represents some of the spanning trees of graph given in fig. 6.1.

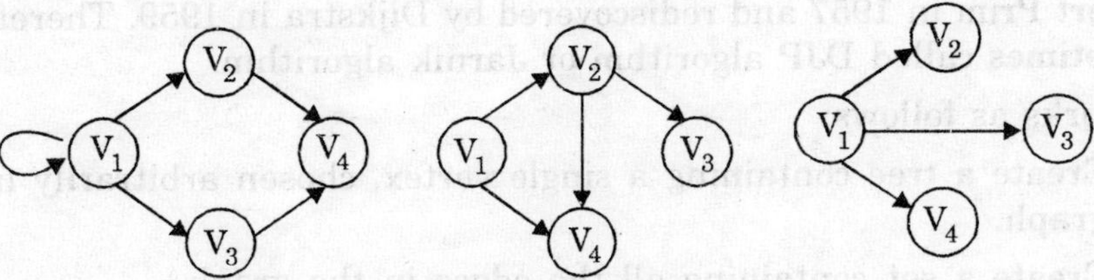

Fig. 6.4 Spanning trees

One example would be a cable TV company laying cable to a new neighborhood. If it is constrained to bury the cable only along certain paths, then there would be a graph representing which points are connected by those paths. Some of those paths might be more expensive, because they are longer, or require the cable to be buried deeper; these paths would be represented by edges with larger weights. A spanning tree for that graph would be a subset of those paths that has no cycles but still connects to every house. There might be several spanning trees possible. A minimum spanning tree would be one with the lowest total cost.

6.4.1 Kruskal's Algorithm

Kruskal's algorithm is an algorithm in graph theory that finds a minimum spanning tree for a connected weighted graph. This means it finds a subset of the edges that forms a tree that includes every vertex, where the total weight of all the edges in the tree is minimized. If the graph is not connected, then it finds a minimum spanning forest (a minimum spanning tree for each connected component). Kruskal's algorithm is an example of a greedy algorithm.

It works as follows:

- Create a forest F (a set of trees), where each vertex in the graph is a separate tree.
- Create a set S containing all the edges in the graph.
- While S is nonempty.
- Remove an edge with minimum weight from S.
- If that edge connects two different trees, then add it to the forest, combining two trees into a single tree.
- otherwise discard that edge.

6.4.2 Prim's Algorithm

Prim's algorithm is an algorithm in graph theory that finds a minimum spanning tree for a connected weighted graph. This means it finds a subset of the edges that forms a tree that includes every vertex, where the total weight of all the edges in the tree is minimized. If the graph is not connected, then it will only find a minimum spanning tree for one of the connected components. The algorithm was discovered in 1930 by mathematician Vojtech Jarnik and later independently by computer scientist Robert Prim in 1957 and rediscovered by Dijkstra in 1959. Therefore it is sometimes called DJP algorithm or Jarnik algorithm.

It works as follows:

- Create a tree containing a single vertex, chosen arbitrarily from the graph.
- Create a set containing all the edges in the graph.
- Loop until every edge in the set connects two vertices in the tree.

- Remove from the set an edge with minimum weight that connects a vertex in the tree with a vertex not in the tree.
- Add that edge to the tree.

Using a simple binary heap data structure, Prim's algorithm can be shown to run in time which is O ((m + n) log n) where m is the number of edges and n is the number of vertices.

6.4.3 Dijkstra's Algorithm

Dijkstra's algorithm, named after its inventor, Dutch computer scientist Edsger Dijkstra, is an algorithm that solves the single-source shortest path problem for a directed graph with nonnegative edge weights.

For example, if the vertices of the graph represent cities and edge weights represent driving distances between pairs of cities connected by a direct road, Dijkstra's algorithm can be used to find the shortest route between two cities.

Description of the algorithm

Dijkstra's algorithm finds the length of an *optimal* path between two vertices in a graph. (*Optimal* can mean *shortest* or *cheapest* or *fastest* or optimal in some other sense: it depends on how you choose to label the edges of the graph.) The algorithm works as follows:

1. Choose the source vertex.
2. Define a set S of vertices, and initialize it to empty set. As the algorithm progresses, the set S will store those vertices to which a shortest path has been found.
3. Label the source vertex with 0, and insert it into S.
4. Consider each vertex not in S connected by an edge from the newly inserted vertex. Label the vertex not in S with the label of the newly inserted vertex + the length of the edge.
   - But if the vertex not in S was already labeled, its new label will be min(label of newly inserted vertex + length of edge, old label).
5. Pick a vertex not in S with the smallest label, and add it to S.
6. Repeat from step 4, until the destination vertex is in S or there are no labeled vertices not in S.

If the destination is labeled, its label is the distance from source to destination. If it is not labeled, there is no path from the source to the destination.

Example:

Consider graph in fig. 6.5, suppose A is the source state. To explain the algorithm, we'll record the sequence of states we are in each time we get to step 4.

1. A has label 0. S={A}.

2. A has label 0, B has 14, D has 22, E has 4. S = {A, E}.
3. A is 0, B has label 14, D has been relabelled 16, F has 14. We inserted F (we could have chosen B instead). S = {A, E, F}.

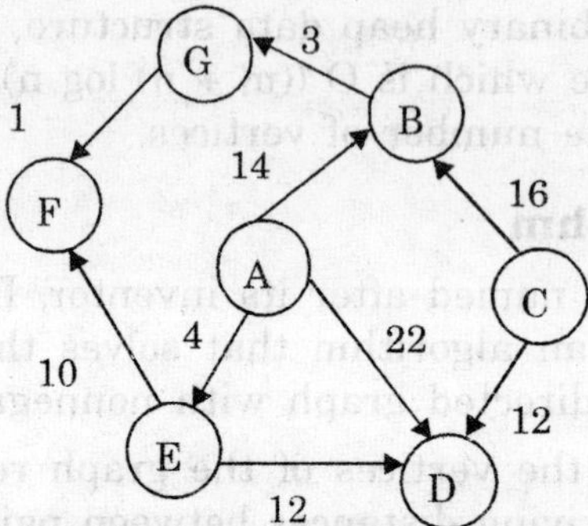

Fig. 6.5 Weighted graph

4. No change to labels. S = {A, E, F, B}.
5. Labels as before and also G has 17. S = {A, E, F, B, D}.
6. No change to labels. S = {A, E, F, B, D, G}.
7. Stop because there are no labeled vertices not in S.

The labels now record the shortest distance from A. (States with no label, such as C, cannot be reached from A.)

Dijkstra's algorithm calculates the *length* of the optimal path. But we can easily generalize it so that it can also give us the path itself. One way to do this is to maintain, along with the label for each node, the previous node we used to get there. Then the path can be extracted by starting at the destination and following the previous-node labels.

Program for shortest path (Dijkstra's) algorithm

```
#include<iostream.h>
#include<stdio.h>
#include<conio.h>
class graph
{
        int len[10][10];
        int dist[10];
        int s[10];
        int size;
        public:
        graph(int s1)
        {
            size=s1;
            for(int i=1;i<=size;i++)
```

```
            for(int j=1;j<=size;j++)
                len[i][j]=1000;
        }
        void get();
        void shortest(const int, const int);
        int choose(const int);
        void print();
};
void graph::shortest(const int n,const int v)
{
    for(int i=1;i<=n;i++)
    {
        s[i]=0;
        dist[i]=len[v][i];
    }
    s[v]=1;
    dist[v]=0;
    for(i=1;i<=n-1;i++)
    {
        int u = choose(n);      cout<<"U is :"<<u<<"\n";
        s[u]=1;
        for(int w=1;w<=n;w++)
            if(!s[w])
                if(dist[u]+len[u][w] < dist[w])
                    dist[w]=len[u][w]+dist[u];
    }
}
int graph::choose(const int n)
{
    int min=500;
    int minp=0;
    for(int i=1;i<=n;i++)
    {
        if((s[i]==0) && (dist[i]<= min))
        {
            min = dist[i];
            minp = i;
```

```
            }
        }
        return(minp);
    }

void graph::print()
{
    cout<<endl;
    for(int i=1;i<=size;i++)
            cout<<dist[i]<<"\t";
    getch();
}
void graph::get()
{
    int a1,i,j,vex,we;
    cout<<"Enter the relation\n";
    for(i=1;i<=size;i++)
    {
            cout<<"Enter the adjacency of "<<i<<"\n";
            cin>>a1;
            if(a1==0)
            {
                    for(j=1;j<=size;j++)
                            len[i][j]=0;
            }
            else
            {
                    for(j=1;j<=a1;j++)
                    {
                            cout<<"Enter the vertex\n";
                            cin>>vex;
                            cout<<"Enter the weight\n";
                            cin>>we;
                            len[i][vex]=we;
                    }
            }
    }
```

```
        cout<<"\nAd. Matrix is :\n";
        for(i=1;i<=size;i++)
        {
            for(j=1;j<=size;j++)
            {
                cout<<len[i][j]<<"\t";
            }
            cout<<endl;
        }
        cout<<endl;
    }

    void main()
    {
        clrscr();
        int c;
        cout<<"Enter the no of node\n";
        cin>>c;
        graph G(c);
        G.get();
        for(int i=1;i<=c;i++)
        {
            cout<<i<<" to All"<<"\n";
            G.shortest(c,i);
            G.print();
        }
    }
```

Exercises

1. Show that the sum of the degrees of the vertices of an undirected graph is twice the number of edges.
2. Draw complete undirected graphs on one, two, three, four and five vertices. Prove that number of edges in an n-vertex complete graph is n (n–1)/2.
3. Write a C++ function for depth-first search under the assumption that graphs are represented using adjacency matrices.
4. Write a C++ function for breadth-first search under the assumption that graphs are represented using adjacency lists.
5. Prove that DFS is applied to a connected graph the edges of T form a tree.
6. Differentiate DFS and BFS.
7. Implement and list the function for determining shortest distances in directed graphs with weights.
8. Write a program that finds
   - The number of vertices in a graph
   - The number of adjacent vertices for a given vertex.
9. Modify the shortest path algorithm, so that it obtains the shortest path and also the length of the path.

7

SORTING AND SEARCHING

7.1 SEARCH

Searching is a process to identify the particular value is available in the given list or not.

7.1.1 Linear Search

Linear search is a search algorithm, also known as sequential search, that is suitable for searching a set of data for a particular value.

It operates by checking every element of a list until a match is found. Linear search runs in O(N). If the data are distributed randomly, on average N/2 comparisons will be needed. The best case is that the value is equal to the first element tested, in which case only 1 comparison is needed. The worst case is that the value is not in the list, in which case N comparisons are needed.

7.1.2 Binary Search

Binary search is a search algorithm for searching a set of sorted data for a particular value. A binary search requires random access to the data being searched. In its simplest form, binary search assumes the data is sorted (usually by a sort algorithm) and takes advantage of that characteristic.

An example of binary search in action is a simple guessing game in which a player has to guess a positive integer selected by another player between 1 and N, using only questions answered with yes or no. Supposing N is 16 and the number 11 is selected, the game might proceed as follows.

- Is the number greater than 8? (Yes)
- Is the number greater than 12? (No)
- Is the number greater than 10? (Yes)
- Is the number greater than 11? (No)

Therefore, the number must be 11. At each step, we choose a number right in the middle of the range of possible values for the number. For example, once we know the number is greater than 8, but less than or equal to 12, we know to choose a number in the middle of the range [9, 12] (either 10 or 11 will do).

At most [$\log_2 N$] questions are required to determine the number, since each question halves the search space. Note that one less question (iteration) is required than for the general algorithm, since the number is constrained to a particular range.

7.1.3 Hashing

If we have a collection of **n** elements whose keys are unique integers in (1,**m**), where **m** >= **n**,

then we can store the items in a *direct address* table, **T[m]**,

where **Ti** is either empty or contains one of the elements of our collection.

Searching a direct address table is clearly an **O(1)** operation:

for a key, **k**, we access $\mathbf{T_k}$,

- If it contains an element, return it,
- If it doesn't then return a NULL.

There are two constraints here, they are the keys must be unique, and the range of the key must be severely bounded.

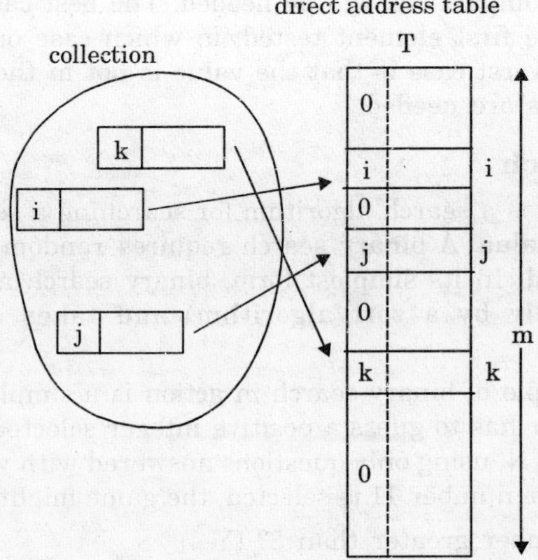

Fig. 7.1 Direct address table

If the keys are not unique, then we can simply construct a set of **m** lists and store the heads of these lists in the direct address table. The time to find an element matching an input key will still be **O(1)**.

7.1.3.1 Hashing function

The direct address approach requires that the function, **h(k)**, is a one-to-one mapping from each **k** to integers in (**1,m**). Such a function is known as a **perfect hashing function**: it maps each key to a distinct integer within some manageable range and enables us to trivially build an **O(1)** search time table.

Unfortunately, finding a perfect hashing function is not always possible. Let's say that we can find a **hash function, h(k)**, which maps *most* of the keys onto unique integers, but maps a small number of keys on to the same integer. If the number of **collisions** (cases where multiple keys map onto the same integer), is sufficiently small, then *hash tables* work quite well and give **O(1)** search times.

7.1.3.2 Handling the collisions

In the small number of cases, where multiple keys map to the same integer, then elements with different keys may be stored in the same "slot" of the hash table. It is clear that when the hash function is used to locate a potential match, it will be necessary to compare the key of that element with the search key. But there may be more than one element which should be stored in a single slot of the table. Various techniques are used to manage this problem:

1. Chaining,
2. Overflow areas,
3. Re-hashing,
4. Using neighbouring slots (linear probing),
5. Quadratic probing,
6. Random probing.

Chaining

One simple scheme is to chain all collisions in lists attached to the appropriate slot. This allows an unlimited number of collisions to be handled and doesn't require a *priori* knowledge of how many elements are contained in the collection.

Re-hashing

Re-hashing schemes use a second hashing operation when there is a collision. If there is a further collision, we *re-hash* until an empty "slot" in the table is found. The re-hashing function can either be a new function or a re-application of the original one.

Linear probing

One of the simplest re-hashing functions is +1 (or –1), *i.e.,* on a collision, look in the neighboring slot in the table. It calculates the new address extremely quickly and may be extremely efficient on a modern RISC processor due to efficient cache utilization.

Linear probing is subject to a **clustering** phenomenon. Re-hashes from one location occupy a block of slots in the table which "grows" towards slots to which other keys hash. This exacerbates the collision problem and the number of re-hashed can become large.

Overflow area

Another scheme will divide the pre-allocated table into two sections: the *primary area* to which keys are mapped and an area for collisions, normally termed the *overflow area*. When a collision occurs, a slot in the overflow area is used for the new element and a link from the primary slot established as in a chained system. This is essentially the same as chaining, except that the overflow area is pre-allocated and thus possibly faster to access. As with re-hashing, the maximum number of elements must be known in advance, but in this case, two parameters must be estimated: the optimum size of the primary and overflow areas.

7.2 SORTING

In computer science and mathematics, a sorting algorithm is an algorithm that puts elements of a list in a certain order. The most used orders are numerical order and lexicographical order. Efficient sorting is important to optimizing the use of other algorithms (such as search and merge algorithms) that require sorted lists to work correctly; it is also often useful for canonicalizing data and for producing human-readable output.

7.2.1 Bubble Sort

Bubble sort is a simple sorting algorithm. It works by repeatedly stepping through the list to be sorted, comparing two items at a time, swapping these two items if they are in the wrong order. The pass through the list is repeated until no swaps are needed, which means the list is sorted. The algorithm gets its name from the way smaller elements "bubble" to the top of the list via the swaps.

Bubble sort needs $O(n^2)$ comparisons to sort n items and can sort in-place. Although the algorithm is one of the simplest sorting algorithms to understand and implement, it is too inefficient for use on lists having more than a few elements.

Bubble sort is asymptotically equivalent in running time to insertion sort, but the two algorithms differ greatly in the number of swaps necessary. In the worst case, bubble sort will require $O(n^2)$ swaps, while insertion sort will require at most O(n) swaps. Naïve implementations of bubble sort (like those below) usually perform badly on already-sorted lists ($O(n^2)$), while insertion sort needs only O(n) operations in this case. Hence many modern algorithm textbooks avoid using the bubble sort algorithm in favor of insertion sort. It is possible to reduce the best case complexity to O(n) if a flag is used to denote whether any swaps were necessary during the first run of the inner loop. In this case, no swaps would indicate an already sorted list. Also, reversing the order in which the list is traversed for each pass improves the efficiency somewhat. This is sometimes called shuttle sort since the algorithm shuttles from one end of the list to the other.

The bubble sort algorithm works as follows:

1. Compare adjacent elements. If the first is greater than the second, swap them.
2. Do this for each pair of adjacent elements, starting with the first two and ending with the last two. At this point the last element should be the greatest.
3. Repeat the steps for all elements except the last one.
4. Keep repeating for one fewer element each time, until you have no more pairs to compare.

As an example, begin with the following array.

7 4 1 9 2

The bubble sort focuses on the first two elements in the array (7 and 4), which are compared and swapped if necessary. In this case, since the element at index 0 is larger than the one at index 1, the values are swapped. Then the focus moves to the elements at index 1 and 2, which are compared and swapped, if necessary. In our example, 7 is larger than 1, so the two elements are swapped. The result is that the largest of the first three elements is now at index 2.

```
Pass 1 :  7 4 1 9 2
          4 7 1 9 2
          4 1 7 9 2
          4 1 7 2 9
Pass 2 :  1 4 7 2 9
          1 4 2 7 9
Pass 3 :  1 2 4 7 9
Pass 4 :  1 2 4 7 9
```

The process is repeated until the focus moves to the end of the array, at which point the largest of all the elements ends up at the highest possible index. In this case, the element 9 will be the last value of the array. Please note that all this results after single iteration. This loop will repeat itself until all values or sorted in increasing order.

Program for bubble sort in C++

```
#include<iostream.h>
#include<conio.h>
#include<stdio.h>
#include<string.h>
class emp
{
    int empno;
    char *name;
```

```
        int age;
        friend employee;
    };
class employee
    {
        int size,i,j;
        emp *database;
        int t,t2;
        char *t1;
        public:
        employee(int s)
        {
            size = s;
                database = new emp[size];
        }
        void create(int,char *,int);
        void print();
        void sort();
    };
void employee::create(int r,char *n,int ag)
{
        static int i=0;
        database[i].empno = r;
        strcpy(database[i].name,n);
        database[i].age=ag;
        i++;
}
void employee::print()
{
        cout<<"Number \t Name \t Age\n";
        for(int i=0;i<size;i++)
        {
            cout<<database[i].empno<<"\t";
            cout<<database[i].name<<"\t";
            cout<<database[i].age<<"\n";
            cout<<endl;
```

```
        }
    }

void employee::sort()
{
    for(i=0;i<size;i++)
      {
        for(j=0;j<size;j++)
          {
              if(database[i].empno < database[j].empno)
              {
                  t = database[i].empno;
                  strcpy(t1,database[i].name);
                  t2=database[i].age;
                  database[i].empno =database[j].empno;
                  strcpy(database[i].name,database[j].name);
                  database[i].age=database[j].age;
                  database[j].empno=t;
                  strcpy(database[j].name,t1);
                  database[j].age=t2;
              }
          }
      }
}

void main()
{
    char *ne;
    int no,ag,n;
    clrscr();
    cout<<"Enter the no of record\n";
    cin>>n;
    employee E(n);
    for(int i=0;i<n;i++)
      {
          cout<<"Enter the name\n";
```

```
            cin>>ne;
            cout<<"Enter the no\n";
            cin>>no;
            cout<<"Enter the Age\n";
            cin>>ag;
            E.create(no,ne,ag);
        }
        cout<<"Given data is :\n";
        E.print();
        E.sort();
        cout<<"After Sorting in Emp No\n";
        E.print();
        getch();
    }
```

7.2.2 Selection Sort

Selection sort is a sort algorithm that works as follows:

1. Find the minimum value in the list.
2. Swap it with the value in the first position.
3. Sort the remainder of the list (excluding the first value).

If you had to invent a sort algorithm on your own, you'd probably write an algorithm similar to selection sort because it is probably the most intuitive and immediate to invent. This algorithm, iterating through a list of n unsorted items, has a worst-case, average-case, and best-case run-time of $\Theta(n^2)$, assuming that comparisons can be done in constant time.

7 4 1 9 2

The selection sort marks the first element (7). It then goes through the remaining data to find the smallest number (1). It swaps with the first element (7) and the smallest element (1), which is placed in its correct position. It then marks the second element (4) and looks through the remaining data for the next smallest number (2). These two numbers are then swapped. Mark the third element (7) and look through the remaining data for the next smallest number (4). These two numbers are now swapped.

```
Pass 1 :  4 7 1 9 2
          1 7 4 9 2
Pass 2 :  1 4 7 9 2
          1 2 7 9 4
Pass 3 :  1 2 4 9 7
Pass 4 :  1 2 4 7 9
```

Lastly it marks the fourth element (9) and looks through the remaining data for the next smallest number (7). These two numbers are then swapped. If we were not finished at this point this sort would continue until n – 1 passes have been made.

Program for Selection Sort

```
#include<iostream.h>
#include<conio.h>
#include<stdio.h>
#include<string.h>
class emp
{
    int empno;
    char *name;
    int age;
    friend employee;
 };
class employee
{
    int size,i,j;
    emp *database;
    int t,t2;
    char *t1;
    public:
    employee(int s)
    {
        size = s;
        database =  new emp[size];
    }
    void create(int,char *,int);
    void print();
    void sort();
};
void employee::create(int r,char *n,int ag)
{
    static int i=0;
    database[i].empno = r;
    strcpy(database[i].name,n);
```

```
        database[i].age=ag;
        i++;
    }
void employee::print()
    {
        cout<<"\t\tEmployee Sorted List\n";
        cout<<"Number \t Name \t Age\n";
        for(int i=0;i<size;i++)
        {
            cout<<database[i].empno<<"\t";
            cout<<database[i].name<<"\t";
            cout<<database[i].age<"\n";
            cout<<endl;
        }

    }
void employee::sort()
    {
        for(i=0;i<size-1;i++)
        {
            for(j=i+1;j<size;j++)
            {
                if(database[i].empno > database[j].empno)
                {
                    t = database[i].empno;
                    strcpy(t1,database[i].name);
                    t2=database[i].age;
                    database[i].empno =database[j].empno;
                    strcpy(database[i].name,database[j].name);
                    database[i].age=database[j].age;
                    database[j].empno=t;
                    strcpy(database[j].name,t1);
                    database[j].age=t2;
                }
            }
        }
    }
```

```
void main()
{
        char *ne;
        int no,ag,n;
        clrscr();
        cout<<"Enter the no of record\n";
        cin>>n;
        employee E(n);
        for(int i=0;i<n;i++)
        {
                cout<<"Enter the name\n";
                cin>>ne;
                cout<<"Enter the no\n";
                cin>>no;
                cout<<"Enter the Age\n";
                cin>>ag;
                E.create(no,ne,ag);
        }
        cout<<"Given data is :\n";
        E.print();
        E.sort();
        cout<<"After Sorting\n";
        E.print();
        getch();
}
```

7.2.3 Insertion Sort

Insertion sort is a simple sort algorithm in which the sorted array (or list) is built one entry at a time. It is much less efficient than the more advanced algorithms such as quick sort, heap sort, or merge sort, but it has various advantages:

- Simple to implement.
- Efficient on (quite) small data sets.
- Efficient on data sets which are already substantially sorted.
- Stable (does not change the order of already ordered elements).
- In-place.
- It is an online algorithm, in that it can sort a list as it receives it.

In abstract terms, each iteration of an insertion sort removes an element from the input data, inserting it at the correct position in the already sorted list, until no elements are left in the input. The choice of which element to remove from the input is arbitrary and can be made using almost any choice algorithm.

The algorithm can be described as :

1. Start with the result being the first element of the input.
2. Loop over the input array until it is empty, "removing" the first remaining (leftmost) element.
3. Compare the removed element against the current result, starting from the highest (rightmost) element, and working left towards the lowest element.
4. If the removed input element is lower than the current result element, copy that value into the following element to make room for the new element below, and repeat with the next lowest result element.
5. Otherwise, the new element is in the correct location; save it in the cell left by copying the last examined result up, and start again from (2) with the next input element.

7.2.4 Quick Sort

Quicksort is a well-known sorting algorithm developed by C. A. R. Hoare that, on average, makes $\Theta(n \log n)$ comparisons to sort n items. However, in the worst-case, it makes $O(n^2)$ comparisons. Typically, quick sort is significantly faster in practice than other $\Theta(n \log n)$ algorithms, because its inner loop can be efficiently implemented on most architectures, and in most real-world data it is possible to make design choices which minimize the possibility of requiring quadratic time.

Quick sort sorts by employing a divide and conquer strategy to divide a list into two sub-lists.

The steps are :

1. Pick an element, called a pivot, from the list.
2. Reorder the list so that all elements which are less than the pivot come before the pivot and so that all elements greater than the pivot come after it (equal values can go either way). After this partitioning, the pivot is in its final position. This is called the partition operation.
3. Recursively sort the sub-list of lesser elements and the sub-list of greater elements.

The base case of the recursion are lists of size zero or one, which are always sorted. The algorithm always terminates because it puts at least one element in its final place on each iteration.

As an example, begin with the following array.

	7 12 6 4 9 5 10 2
Pass 1 :	7 2 6 4 9 5 10 12
	7 2 6 4 5 9 10 12
	[5 2 6 4] 7 [9 10 12]
Pass 2 :	5 2 4 6
	[4 2] 5 [6]
Pass 3 :	[2] 4
Pass 4 :	9 [10 12]
Pass 5 :	10 [12]
Result :	2 4 5 6 7 9 10 12

Performance Details

Quick sort's inner loop, which performs the partition, is amenable to optimization on typical modern machines for two main reasons:

- All comparisons are being done with a single pivot value, which can be stored in a register.
- The list is being traversed sequentially, which produces very good locality of reference and cache behavior for arrays.

This close fit with modern architectures makes quick sort one of the fastest sorting algorithms on average. Because of this excellent average performance and simple implementation, quicksort has become one of the most popular sorting algorithms in practical use.

Although it is often believed to work in-place, quick sort uses O(log n) additional stack space on average in recursive implementations and O(n) stack space in the worst case.

The most crucial concern of a quick sort implementation is the choosing of a good pivot element. A naïve implementation of quicksort, like the ones below, will be terribly inefficient for certain inputs. For example, if the input is already sorted, a common practical case, this implementation of quick sort degenerates into a selection sort with $O(n^2)$ running time. Furthermore, the recursion depth becomes linear, requiring O(n) extra stack space.

Program for Quick Sort in C++

```
#include<iostream.h>
#include<conio.h>
#include<stdio.h>
class qsort
{
        int *a;
        int size;
```

```
public:
qsort(){}
qsort(int s)
{
    size = s;
    a = new int[size];
}
void get();
void put();
void sort();
void qqsort(int,int);
};
void qsort::get()
{
    for(int i=0;i<size;i++)
    cin>>a[i];
}
void qsort::put()
{
    for(int i=0;i<size;i++)
    cout<<a[i]<<"\t";
}
void qsort::sort()
{
    get();
    cout<<"Given is :\n";
    put();
    qqsort(0,size-1);
    cout<<"\n\nAfter Sorting\n";
    put();
}
void qsort::qqsort(int l,int u)
{
    int key = a[l];
    int i,j;
    i=l+1;
    j=u;
```

```
        if(l<u)
        {
            while(i<j)
            {
                while(key > a[i])
                    i++;
                while(key < a[j])
                    j--;
                if(i<j)
                {
                    int t=a[i];
                    a[i]=a[j];
                    a[j]=t;
                }
            }
            int t =a[l];
            a[l] = a[j];
            a[j]=t;
            qqsort(l,j-1);
            qqsort(j+1,u);
        }
    }

    void main()
    {
        clrscr();
        int n;
        cout<<"Enter the size of array\n";
        cin>>n;
        qsort q(n);
        q.sort();
        getch();
    }
```

7.2.5 Merge Sort

Merge sort is a sort algorithm for rearranging lists (or any other data structure that can only be accessed sequentially, e.g. file streams) into a specified order. It is a particularly good example of the divide and conquer algorithmic paradigm.

Algorithm

Conceptually, merge sort works as follows :

1. Divide the unsorted list into two sublists of about half the size.
2. Sort each of the two sublists.
3. Merge the two sorted sublists back into one sorted list.

Analysis

Merge sort has an average and worst-case performance of O(n log n). In the worst case, merge sort does about 30% fewer comparisons than quick sort does in the average case; thus merge sort very often needs to make fewer comparisons than quick sort. In terms of moves, merge sort's worst case complexity is O(n log n)—the same complexity as quicksort's best case, and merge sort's best case takes about half as much time as the worst case.

However, merge sort performs 2n – 1 method calls in the worst case, compared to quick sort's n, thus has roughly twice as much recursive overhead as quicksort. Mergesort's most common implementation does not sort in place, meaning memory the size of the input must be allocated for the sorted output to be stored in. Sorting in-place is possible but requires an extremely complicated implementation.

Merge can also be used for a variety of other things :

- Given a set of current account balances and a set of transactions, both sorted by account number, produce the set of new account balances after the transactions are applied; this requires always advancing the "new transactions" pointer in preference to the "account number" pointer when the two have equal keys, and adding all the numbers on either tape with the same account number to produce the new balance.
- Produce a sorted list of records with keys present in all the lists (equijoin); this requires outputting a record whenever the keys of all the $p_{0..n}$ are equal.
- Similarly for finding the largest number on one tape smaller than each number on another tape (e.g., to figure out what tax bracket each person is in).
- Similarly for computing set differences: all the records in one list with no corresponding records in another.

Example:

7 12 6 4 9 5 10 2

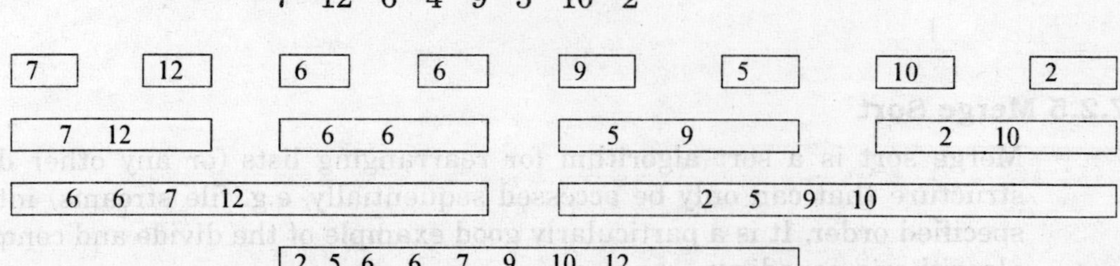

Program for Merge Sort in C++

```
#include<iostream.h>
#include<conio.h>
#include<stdio.h>
class merge
{
    int *a,*b;
    int size;
    public:
    merge(int s){size=s;a = new int[size];b = new int[size];}
    void get();
    void put();
    void sort();
    void mergesort(int,int);
    void merge1(int,int,int);
};
void merge::get()
{
    cout<<"Enter the elements\n";
    for(int i=0;i<size;i++)
    {
        cin>>a[i]; b[i]=0;
    }
}
void merge::put()
{
    cout<<"Sorting the Elements:\n";
    for(int i=0;i<size;i++)
        cout<<b[i]<<"\t";
}
void merge::mergesort(int l,int h)
{
    if(l < h)
    {
        int mid = (l+h)/2;
        mergesort(l,mid);
        mergesort(mid+1,h);
        merge1(l,mid,h);
```

```
        }
    }
void merge::merge1(int l,int m,int h)
 {
        int i=l;
         int j= m+1;
        int p=l;
        while((i<=m) && (j<=h))
        {
                if(a[i] <= a[j])
                {
                        b[p]=a[i];
                        i=i+1; p++;
                }
                else
                {
                        b[p]=a[j];
                        j=j+1; p++;
                }
         }
        if(i>m)
        {
                for(int k=j;k<=h;k++)
                {
                        b[p]=a[k];
                        p=p+1;
                }
        }
        else if(j>h)
        {
                for(int k=i;k<=m;k++)
                {
                        b[p]=a[k];
                        p=p+1;
                }
        }
        for(int k=l;k<=h;k++)
                a[k]=b[k];
```

```
}
void merge::sort()
{
      get();
      mergesort(0,size-1);
      put();
}

void main()
{
      clrscr();
      cout<<"Program for Merge Sort\n";
      cout<<"~~~~~~~~ ~~~ ~~~~~ ~~~~\n";
       int n;
      cout<<"Enter the no of elements\n";
      cin>>n;
      merge M(n);
      M.sort();
      getch();
}
```

7.2.6 Heap Sort

Heap is a complete binary tree such that the weight of every node is less than the weights of its children. One simple way to sort a list of objects is to use a heap data structure. We add all of our objects into the heap, and the heap organizes the elements added to it in such a way that we can quickly extract either the largest value (in a max-heap) or the smallest value (in a min-heap). Moreover, because this operation preserves the heap's structure, we can extract the largest/smallest value over and over again until none remain. This gives us the elements in order.

A heap with n elements can be conveniently represented as the first n elements of an array. Furthermore, the children of $a[i]$ can be found in $a[2i]$ (left child) and $a[2i + 1]$ (right child).

The sort algorithm works as follows :

```
Insert all records to form a heap S;
while (S is not empty)
      {
            y = max (S);
            Size of S called n becomes n–1
      }
```

Example:

The Initial Array is : 7 12 4 9 5 10 2

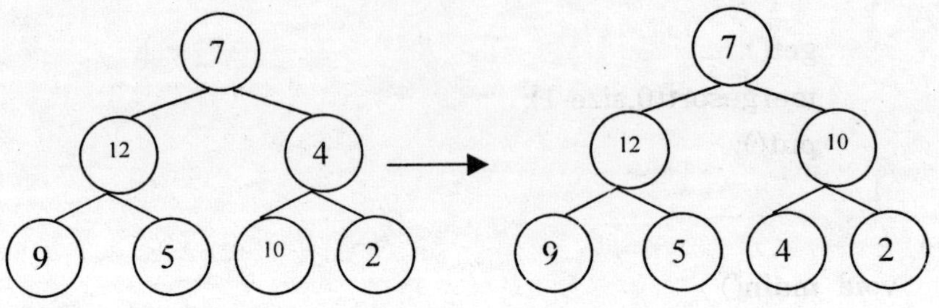

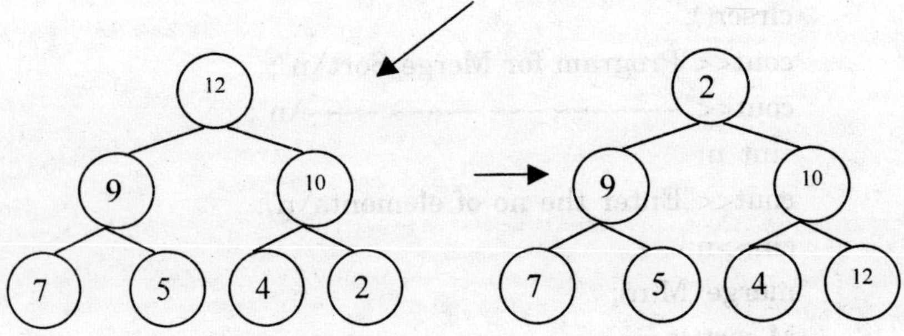

Initial Heap

Heap: _______ 12

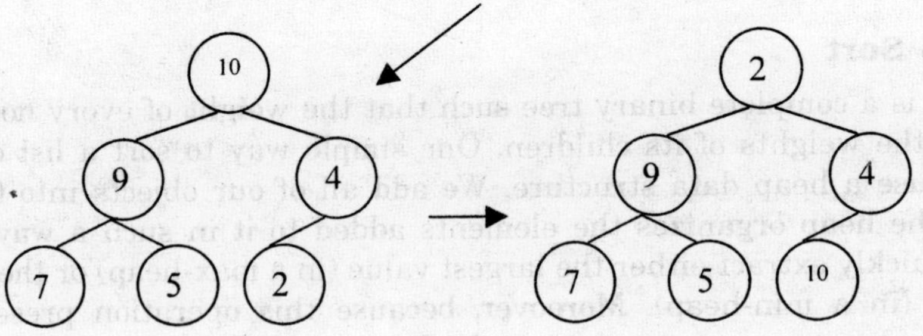

Heap: _____ 10 12

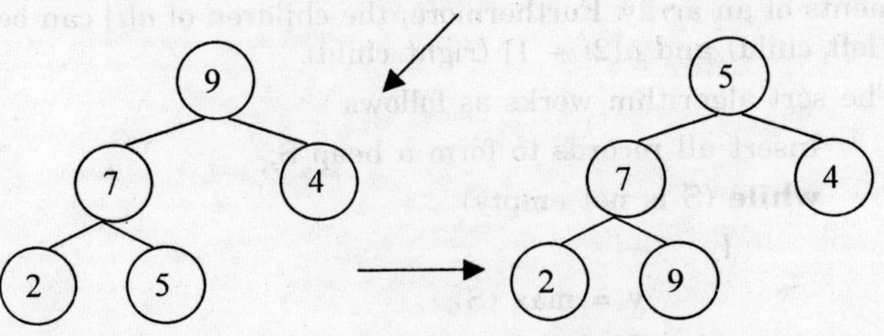

Heap: ____ 9 10 12

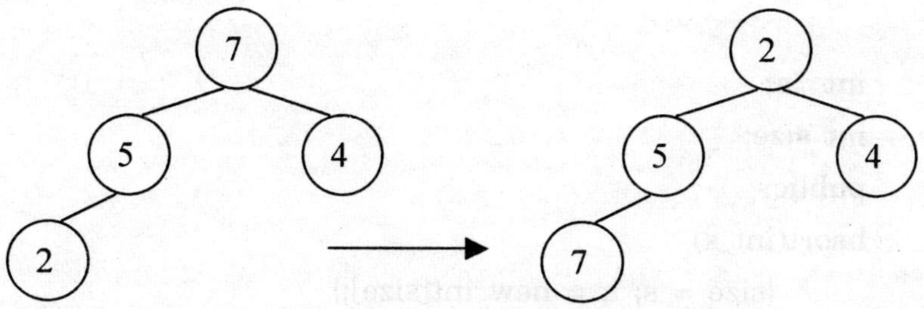

Heap: _ _ _ 7 9 10 12

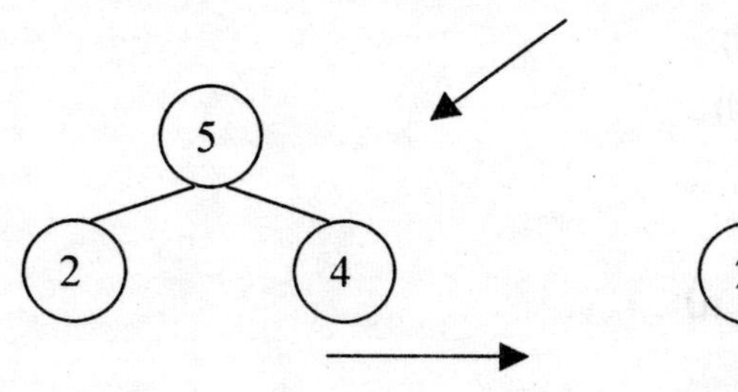

Heap: _ _ 5 7 9 10 12

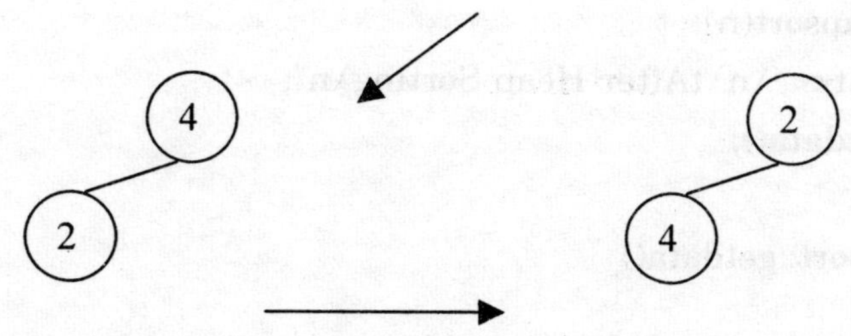

Heap: _ 4 5 7 9 10 12

Heap: 2 4 5 7 9 10 12

Program for Heap Sort

```
#include<iostream.h>
#include<conio.h>
#include<stdio.h>
class hsort
```

```
{
      int *a;
      int size;
      public:
      hsort(int s)
            {size = s; a = new int[size];}
      void heapsort(int);
      void adjust(int,int);
      void getdata();
      void putdata();
      void sort(int);
 };
void hsort::sort(int n)
 {
      getdata();
      cout<<"Given Elements is :\n";
      putdata();
      heapsort(n);
      cout<<"\n\tAfter Heap Sorting\n";
      putdata();
 }
 void hsort::getdata()
 {
      for(int i=1;i<=size;i++)
       cin>>a[i];
 }
 void hsort::putdata()
 {
      for(int i=1;i<=size;i++)
       cout<<a[i]<<" ";
 }
 void hsort::heapsort(int n)
 {
      for(int i=n/2;i>=1;i--)
            adjust(i,n);
      for(i=n-1;i>=1;i--)
```

```
        {
            int t=a[i+1];
            a[i+1]=a[1];
            a[1]=t;
            adjust(1,i);
        }
    }
void hsort::adjust(int r,int n)
{
    int e = a[r];
    for(int j=2*r;j<=n;j=j*2)
    {
        if(j<n)
            if(a[j] < a[j+1]) j++;
        if(e >= a[j])
            break;
        else
            a[j/2] = a[j];
    }
    a[j/2] = e;
}

void main()
{
    clrscr();
    cout<<"Enter the no of Elements\n";
    int el;
    cin>>el;
    hsort H(el);
    H.sort(el);
    getch();
}
```

Exercises

1. Write a non-recursive function for binary search.
2. On average, about how may more comparisons does selection sort do than insertion sort on a list of 20 items?
3. Explain why merge sort is better for linked lists than for contiguous lists.
4. Show that the worst-case time complexity of Quick sort is $O(n^2)$.
5. Write a non-recursive function for quick sort.
6. What is the worst case complexity of bubble sort function?
7. Obtain an algorithm for a two-way merge sort using linked allocation techniques.

8

SEARCH TREES

8.1 HEIGHT BALANCED TREE

A self-balancing binary search tree or height-balanced binary search tree is a binary search tree that attempts to keep its height, or the number of levels of nodes beneath the root, as small as possible at all times, automatically. This is important, because most operations on a binary search tree take time directly proportional to the tree's height. They are one of the most efficient ways of implementing associative arrays, and other data structures.

Ordinary binary search trees have the primary disadvantage that they can attain very large heights in rather ordinary situations, such as when the keys are inserted in order. The result is a data structure similar to a linked list, making all operations on the tree expensive. Self-balancing binary trees solve this problem by performing transformations on the tree, such as tree rotations, at key times, in order to reduce the height. Although a certain overhead is involved, it is typically spread across many operations.

8.2 AVL TREE

An AVL tree is the first invented self-balancing binary search tree. In an AVL tree the height of the two child subtrees of any node differ by at most one, therefore it is also known as height-balanced. Lookup, insertion, and deletion are all O(log n) in both the average and worst cases. Additions and deletions may require the tree to be rebalanced by one or more tree rotations.

The balance factor of a node is the height of its right subtree minus the height of its left subtree. A node with balance factor 1, 0, or –1 is considered balanced. A node with balance factor –2 or 2 is considered unbalanced and requires rebalancing the tree. The balance factor is either stored directly at each node or computed from the heights of the subtrees, possibly stored at nodes.

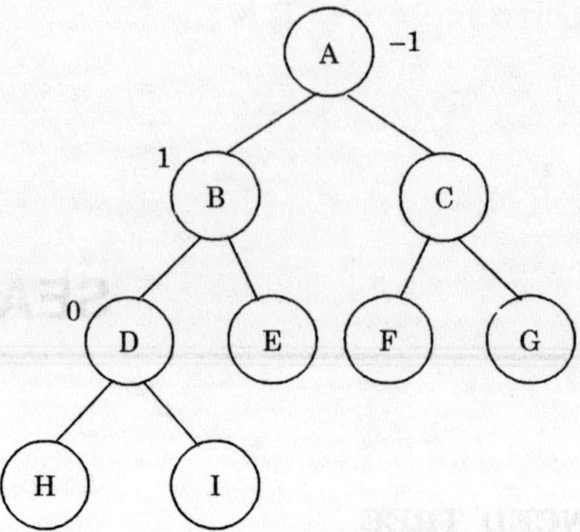

Fig. 8.1 AVL tree

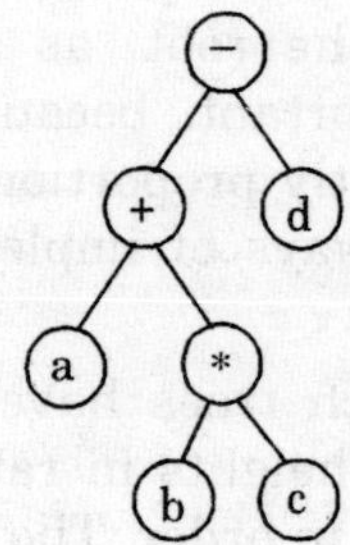

Fig. 8.2 Non-AVL tree

8.2.1 Single Right Rotation (SRR)

```
      A        SRR at A        B
     / \      ---------->     / \
    B   T3                  T1   A
   / \                          / \
 T1   T2                      T2   T3
```

A is the node that the rotation is performed on. This rotation is performed when A is unbalanced to the left (the left sub tree is 2 higher than the right sub tree) and B is left heavy (the left sub tree of B is 1 higher than the right sub tree of B). T1, T2 and T3 represent sub trees (a node was added to T1 which made B left heavy and unbalanced A).

8.2.2 Single Left Rotation (SLR)

A is the node that the rotation is performed on. This rotation is performed when A is unbalanced to the right (the right sub tree is 2 higher than the left sub tree) and B is right heavy (the right sub tree of B is 1 higher than the left sub tree of B). T1, T2 and T3 represent sub trees (a node was added to T3 which made B right-heavy and unbalanced A).

```
      A        SLR at A          B
     / \      ---------->       / \
   T1   B                      A   T3
       / \                    / \
     T2   T3                T1   T2
```

8.2.3 Double Left Rotation (DLR)

C is the node that the rotation is performed on. This rotation is performed when C is unbalanced to the left (the left sub tree is 2 higher than the right sub tree), A is right heavy (the right sub tree of A is 1 higher than the left sub tree of A) and B is left-heavy. T1, T2, T3, and T4 represent sub trees (a node was added to T2 which made B left-heavy, made A right-heavy and unbalanced C). This consists of a single left rotation at node A, followed by a single right at node C.

```
         A                        C                          C
        / \     SLR at A         / \       SRR at           / \
       A  T4   ---------->      B  T4     ---------->      A   C
      / \                      / \                        / \  / \
     T1  B                    A  T3                     T1 T2 T3 T4
        / \                  / \
      T2  T3               T1  T2
```

That is,

DLR equiv SLR + SRR

8.2.4 Double Right Rotation (DRR)

A is the node that the rotation is performed on. This rotation is performed when A is unbalanced to the right (the right sub tree is 2 higher than the left sub tree), C is left heavy (the left sub tree of C is 1 higher than the right sub tree of C) and B is right-heavy. T1, T2, T3, and T4 represent sub trees (a node was added to T3 which made B right-heavy, made C left-heavy and unbalanced A). This consists of a single right at node C, followed by a single left at node A.

The basic operations of an AVL tree generally involve carrying out the same algorithms as would be carried out on an unbalanced binary search tree, but preceded or followed by one or more of the so-called "AVL rotations."

```
      A                      A                        B
     / \     SRR at C       / \      SLR at A        / \
    T1  C   ---------->    T1  B    ---------->     A   C
       / \                    / \                  / \  / \
      B  T4                  T2  C               T1 T2 T3 T4
     / \                        / \
    T2 T3                      T3 T4
```

That is,

DRR equiv SRR + SLR

8.3 MULTI WAY SEARCH TREE

As we saw in the previous section, the AVL tree is a binary tree ADT which permits good performance for search, insertion and deletions at the expense of maintaining perfect balance—only "almost balancing" was the compromise.

Another way to compromise on the goal of achieving perfect balance is to permit more than one search key in each node.

In this case, it is possible to arrange all sub trees to be perfectly balanced.

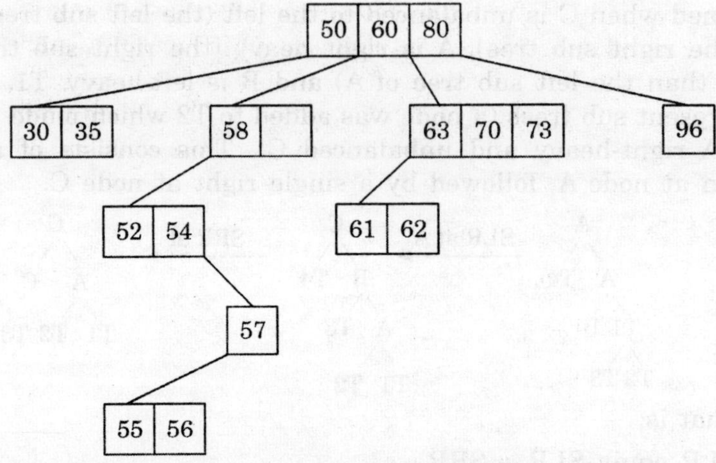

Fig. 8.3 Multi-way search tree

Multi-way (or *m-way*) trees allow multiple keys in each node :

1. Each node has *m* children and *m–1* keys.
2. The keys in each node are in ascending order.
3. The keys in the first *i* children are smaller than the *i*th key.
4. The keys in the last *m–i* children are larger than the *i*th key.

Example 4-way tree :

This makes it simple for key searching.

8.4 2-3 TREE

One simple *balanced m*-way tree is the 2-3 tree :

- Has nodes containing one or two search keys—*i.e.*, each node can have either two or three descendants.
- All leaves are at the same level.

It is called a m-way tree of "order 3".

Example 2-3 tree:

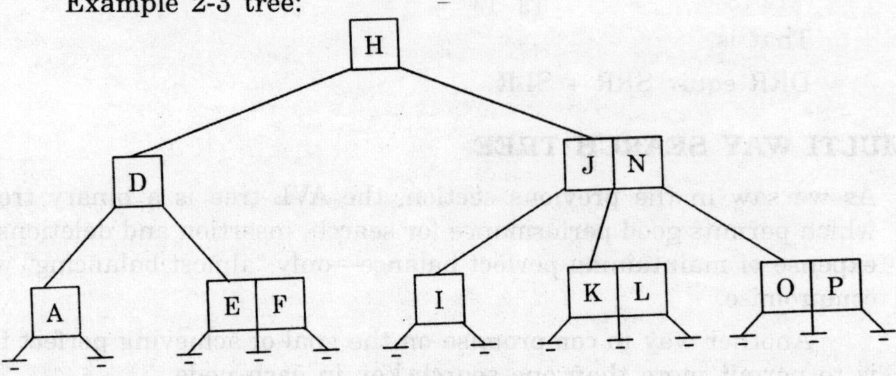

Fig. 8.4 2-3 tree

Since a 2-3 tree has always as many nodes as a full binary tree, a 2-3 tree of height h and N nodes has always at least

$2^h - 1$

Nodes or, alternatively, has a height greater than

Ceiling $(\log_2 (N + 1))$

8.5 2-3-4 TREE

Another simple *balanced* m-way tree is the 2-3-4 tree:

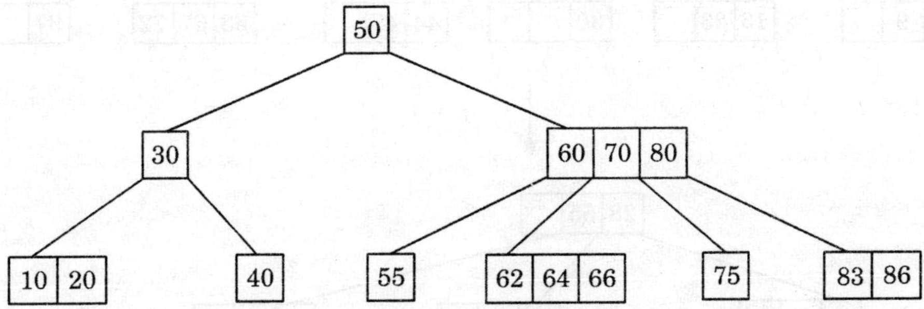

Fig. 8.5 2-3-4 tree

We consider the 2-3-4 tree as they have more efficient insertion and deletion operations than a 2-3 tree, and also serve as a good introduction to B-trees.

Since 2-3-4 trees can have up to 4 children per node, the height of a *full* 2-3-4 tree with N nodes would be

$\log_4 N$

Which is only different by a constant (half) term from the height of a red-black or AVL tree that is full.

Also, there are more items to examine in each node—which, if linear search is used in a node (with, say, requiring a search time equal to M per node), the search time is proportional to

$M^* \log_4 N$

For a 2-3-4 tree that is not full, an average value for M is 2.

That is, $O(M^* \log_4 N) = O(\log N)$ for search.

Which is similar to red-black or AVL trees.

Insertion in a 2-3-4 tree

New data items are always inserted in the leaves of the tree.

The tree is traversed searching for the appropriate leaf node to insert the new key.

Depending on whether a full node is encountered during the search, three cases arise :

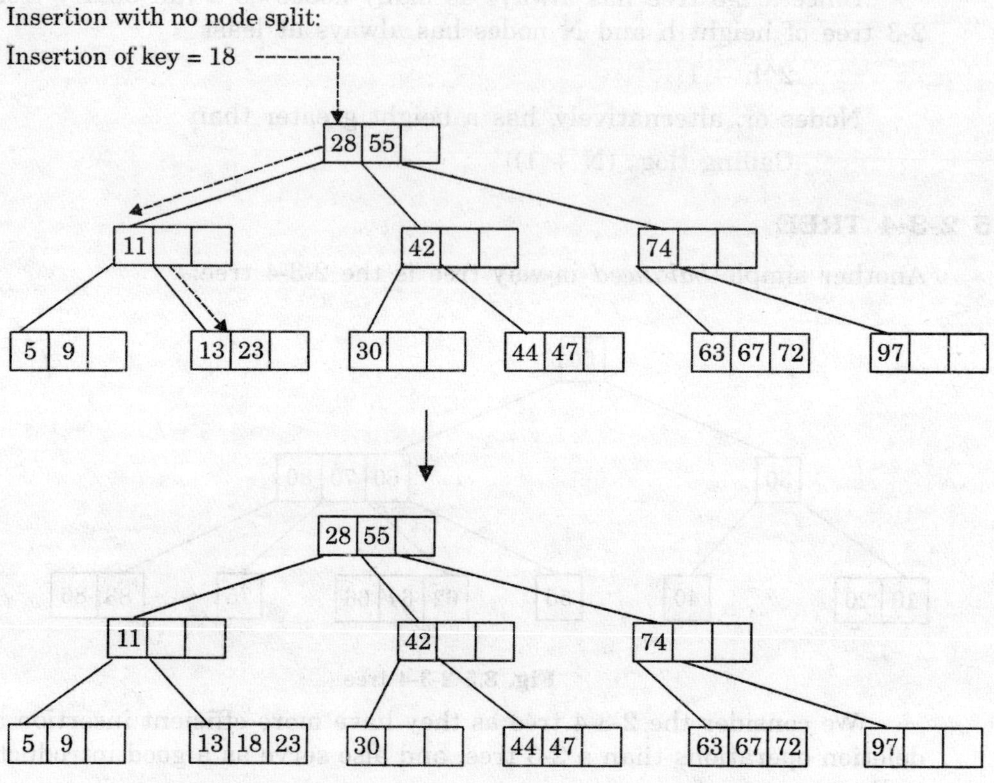

Fig. 8.6 Node insertion in to a 2-3-4 tree with out node split

1. Insertion with no node split.
2. Insertion with node split.
3. Insertion with root node split.

Insertion with no node split

Here, no full nodes are encountered on the path to the leaf node.

Insertion with node split

Here, a full node is encountered on the path to the leaf node and a node split is required.

Multiple splits may be required if more than one full node is encountered on the way down the tree.

It is the splitting process that keeps the tree balanced.

Insertion with root node split

This occurs when a full root is encountered at the beginning of the search. The root 4-node is split into three 2-nodes.

Insertion with a node split:

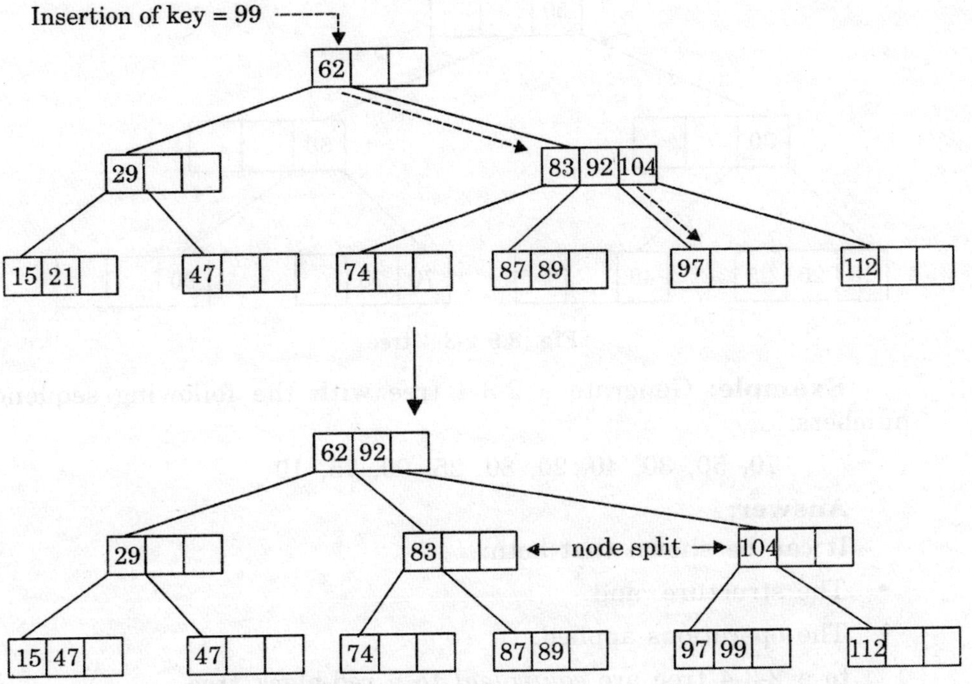

Fig. 8.7 Node insertion in to a 2-3-4 tree with node split

Insertion with a root node split:

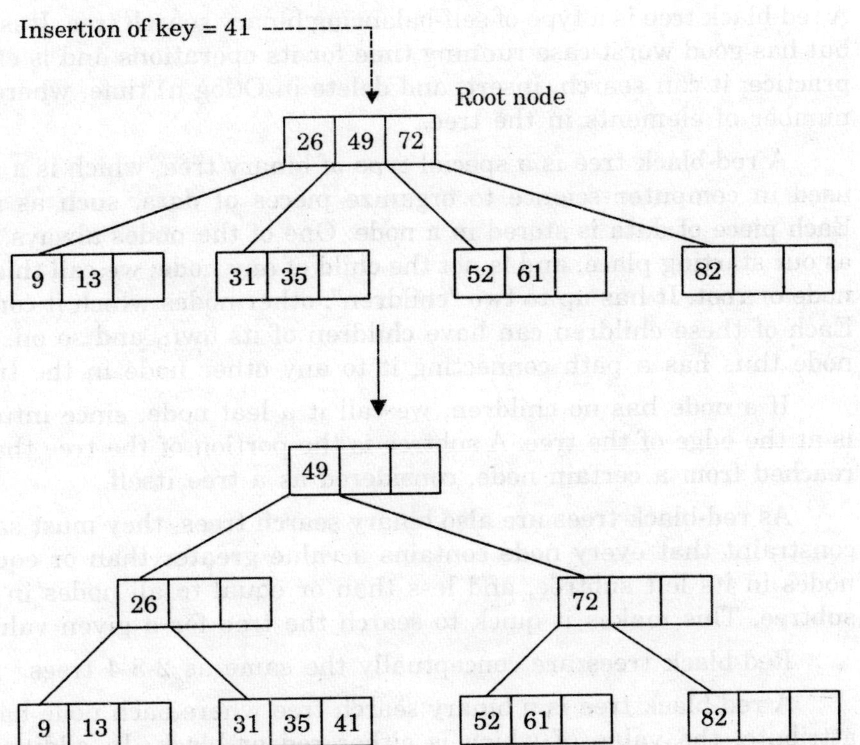

Fig. 8.8 Node insertion in to a 2-3-4 tree root without node split

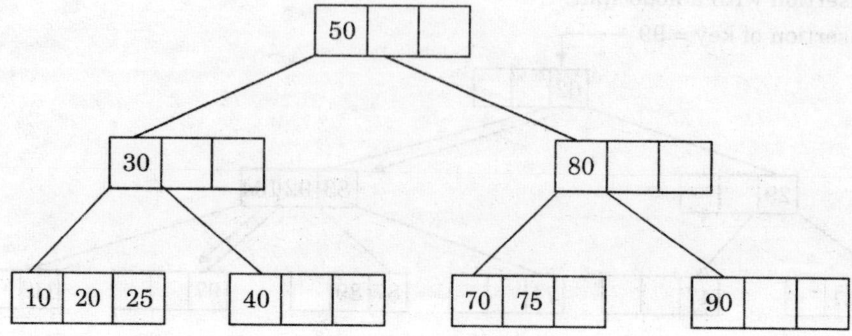

Fig. 8.9 2-3-4 tree

Example: Generate a 2-3-4 tree with the following sequence of numbers:

70, 50, 30, 40, 20, 80, 25, 90, 75, 10

Answer:

It can be shown that both:

- The structure, and
- The operations applied.

to a 2-3-4 tree are *equivalent* to a red-black tree.

8.6 RED-BLACK TREE

A red-black tree is a type of self-balancing binary search tree. It is complex, but has good worst-case running time for its operations and is efficient in practice: it can search, insert, and delete in O(log n) time, where n is the number of elements in the tree.

A red-black tree is a special type of binary tree, which is a structure used in computer science to organize pieces of data, such as numbers. Each piece of data is stored in a node. One of the nodes always functions as our starting place, and is not the child of any node; we call this the root node or root. It has up to two "children", other nodes which it connects to. Each of these children can have children of its own, and so on. The root node thus has a path connecting it to any other node in the tree.

If a node has no children, we call it a leaf node, since intuitively it is at the edge of the tree. A subtree is the portion of the tree that can be reached from a certain node, considered as a tree itself.

As red-black trees are also binary search trees, they must satisfy the constraint that every node contains a value greater than or equal to all nodes in its left subtree, and less than or equal to all nodes in its right subtree. This makes it quick to search the tree for a given value.

Red-black trees are conceptually the same as 2-3-4 trees.

A red-black tree is a binary search tree where each node has a color attribute, the value of which is either red or black. In addition to the ordinary requirements imposed on binary search trees, we make the following additional requirements of any valid red-black tree:

1. A node is either red or black.
2. The root is black.
3. All leaves are black (or null).
4. Both children of each red node are black.
5. The paths from each leaf up to the root contain the same number of black nodes.

These constraints enforce a critical property of red-black trees: that the longest possible path from the root to a leaf is no more than twice as long as the shortest possible path. The result is that the tree is roughly balanced. Since operations such as inserting, deleting and finding values requires worst-case time proportional to the height of the tree, this theoretical upper bound on the height allows red-black trees to be efficient in the worst-case, unlike ordinary binary search trees.

To see why these properties guarantee this, it suffices to note that no path can have two red nodes in a row, due to property 4. The shortest possible path has all black nodes, and the longest possible path alternates between red and black nodes. Since all maximal paths have the same number of black nodes, by property 5, this shows that no path is more than twice as long as any other path.

8.7 SPLAY TREE

A splay tree is a self-balancing binary search tree with the additional unusual property that recently accessed elements are quick to access again. It performs basic operations such as insertion, look-up and removal in O(log(n)) amortized time. For many non-uniform sequences of operations, splay trees perform better than other search trees, even when the specific pattern of the sequence is unknown. The splay tree was invented by Daniel Sleator and Robert Tarjan.

All normal operations on a splay tree are combined with one basic operation, called splaying. Splaying the tree for a certain element rearranges the tree so that the element is placed at the root of the tree. One way to do this is to first perform a standard binary tree search for the element in question, and then use tree rotations in a specific fashion to bring the element to the top. Alternatively, a bottom-up algorithm can combine the search and the tree reorganization.

Advantages

Good performance for a splay tree depends on the fact that it is self-balancing, and indeed self optimising, in that frequently accessed nodes will move nearer to the root where they can be accessed more quickly. This is an advantage for nearly all practical applications, and is particularly useful for implementing caches; however, it is important to note that for uniform access, a splay tree's performance will be considerably (although not asymptotically) worse than a somewhat balanced simple binary search tree.

Splay trees also have the advantage of being considerably simpler to implement than other self-balancing binary search trees, such as red-black trees, or AVL trees, while their average-case performance is just as efficient. Also, splay trees don't need to store any book keeping data, thus minimizing memory requirements. However, these other data structures provide worst-case time guarantees, and can be more efficient in practice for uniform access.

8.8 B-TREES

B-trees are tree data structures that are most commonly found in databases and file systems. B-trees keep data sorted and allow amortized logarithmic time insertions and deletions. B-trees generally grow from the bottom up as elements are inserted, whereas most binary trees grow down.

B-trees have substantial advantages over alternative implementations when node access times far exceed access times within nodes. This usually occurs when most nodes are in secondary storage such as hard drives. By maximizing the number of child nodes within each internal node, the height of the tree decreases, balancing occurs less often, and efficiency increases. Usually this value is set such that each node takes up a full disk block or an analogous size in secondary storage.

The idea behind B-trees is that inner nodes can have a variable number of child nodes within some pre-defined range. Hence, B-trees do not need re-balancing as frequently as other self-balancing binary search trees. The lower and upper bounds on the number of child nodes are fixed for a particular implementation. For example, in a 2-3 B-tree (often simply 2-3 tree), each internal node may have only 2 or 3 child nodes. A node is considered to be in an illegal state if it has an invalid number of child nodes.

8.8.1 Node Structures

Nodes in a B-Tree are usually represented as an ordered set of elements and child pointers. Every node but the root contains a minimum of L elements, a maximum of U elements, and a maximum of U + 1 child pointers, for some arbitrary L and U. For all internal nodes, the number of child pointers is always one more than the number of elements. Since all leaf nodes are at the same height, nodes do not generally contain a way of determining whether they are leaf or internal.

Each inner node's elements act as separation values which divide its subtrees. For example, if an inner node has three child nodes (or subtrees) then it must have two separation values or elements a_1 and a_2. All values in the leftmost subtree will be less than a_1, all values in the middle subtree will be between a_1 and a_2, and all values in the rightmost subtree will be greater than a_2.

8.8.2 Search

Search is performed in the typical manner, analogous to that in a binary search tree. Starting at the root, the tree is traversed top to bottom, choosing the child pointer whose separation values are on either side of the value that is being searched. Binary search is typically used within nodes to determine this location.

8.8.3 Insertion

For a node to be in an illegal state, it must contain a number of elements which is outside of the acceptable range.

1. First, search for the position into which the node should be inserted. Then, insert the value into that node.
2. If no node is in an illegal state then the process is finished.
3. If some node has too many elements, it is split into two nodes, each with the minimum amount of elements. This process continues recursively up the tree until the root is reached. If the root is split, a new root is created. Typically the minimum and maximum number of elements must be selected such that the minimum is no more than one half the maximum in order for this to work.

   Consider the insertion of the following data items into a B-tree of degree 5:

   20, 40, 60, 80, 70, 10, 30, 15, 75, 85, 90, 25, 35, 50, 22, 27, 32

Insertion in order-5 B-tree:

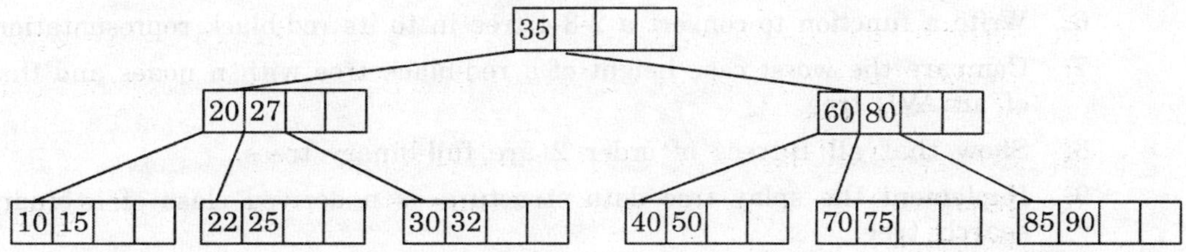

Fig. 8.10 B-Tree of order 5

Notice that no node (except the root) is ever less than 50% full—this is efficient (since we have to keep the nodes as full as possible, but not too full to avoid too many repeated splits).

8.8.4 Deletion

1. First, search for the value which will be deleted. Then, remove the value from the node which contains it.
2. If no node is in an illegal state then the process is finished.
3. If some node is in an illegal state then there are two possible cases:
   1. Its sibling node, a child of the same parent node, can transfer one or more of its child nodes to the current node and return it to a

legal state. If so, after updating the separation values of the parent and the two siblings the process is finished.

2. Its sibling does not have an extra child because it is on the lower bound. In that case both siblings are merged into a single node and we recurse onto the parent node, since it has had a child node removed. This continues until the current node is in a legal state or the root node is reached, upon which the root's children are merged and the merged node becomes the new root.

Exercises

1. Write a C++ function to delete a node from an AVL tree, following the steps in the text.
2. Estimate, how many rotations are needed to insert an item and to delete an item from an AVL tree?
3. What happens when an attempt is made to insert a new key into a full node of a B-tree?
4. In deleting a key from B-tree when is it necessary to combine nodes?
5. Insert the keys below, in the order given into an initially empty B-tree of order

   (a) 3 (*b*) 4 (*c*) 7

   The elements are

   a g f b k d h m j e s I r x c l n t u p
6. Write a function to convert a 2-3-4 tree in to its red-black representation.
7. Compare the worst case height of a red-black tree with n nodes and that of an AVL tree.
8. Show that all B-trees of order 2 are full-binary trees.
9. Implement the splay tree data structure as a derived class of a binary search tree.

INDEX

K

L

M

N

O

P

Q

R

S

T

W